生命中一直在等待的那一天

[美] 弗罗伊德·戴尔 等著

张白桦 译

挚情卷（中英双语）

世界微型小说精选

中国国际广播出版社

自 序

微型小说，又名小小说，今天已经成长为一个独立的文体。作为小说"四大家族"之一，微型小说进入"蒲松龄文学奖"和"鲁迅文学奖"的视野，成为当代受众范围最广的纯文学样式。这一成就的取得，与当代外国微型小说的汉译有着直接的关系。对此，我在《当代外国微型小说汉译的翻译文学意义》的论文中有过详尽的阐述。具体说来，这种新型的、活力四射的文学样式的引进，推动了中国当代主流文学重归文学性，重塑了当代主流诗学，提高了文学的地位，从而创造了民族文学史、国别文学史上的"神话"，具有翻译文学意义。

微型小说翻译对于我来说，好像"量身定制"一般。20世纪80年代初，微型小说在中国横空出世，这种简约而不简单的文体非常适合我的审美取向和性格特征，而翻译则可以调动起我全部的知识和双语语言积累。从1987年我发表的第一篇微型小说译作《他活着还是死了》，到2004年的《我是怎样把心丢了的》，这十七年间，我完成的微型小说翻译总计约350万字。

我的微型小说创作有三种：第一种是母语原创，如《白衣女郎》。第二种是汉译英，如在加拿大出版的《中国微型小说精选》（凌鼎年卷），这是中国第一部英译微型小说自选集，我曾参与翻译。第三种是英译汉，这一种类所占比重最大。代表作有《爱旅无涯》《仇家》《爱你至深》等。

我翻译时的期待视野定位在青年身上，目的是做文化、文学的"媒"，因此更愿意贴近读者，特别是青年读者，觉得"大家好才是真的好"。在翻译策略上以归化为主，异化为辅；在翻译方法上以意译为主，直译为辅；在翻译方式上以全译为主，节译为辅；在翻译风格上以时代性为特色，笃信"一代人有一代人的翻译"之说。

所幸这样的取向还是与读者和社会的需求相契合的，因而产生了一定的社会效益。首译都会发表在国内的百强、十佳报刊，如《读者》《中外期刊文萃》《微型小说选刊》《小小说选刊》《青年参考》《文学故事报》等。常见的情况是，在这样的权威报刊发表后，随即就会呈现"凡有井水处，即能歌柳词"的景观，如《爱你至深》发表的二十年间就被转载60余次。

转载不仅限于报刊之间，数十种权威专辑和选本的纸质版也有收录，如《21世纪中国文学大系翻译文学》、《外国微型小说三百篇》、《世界微型小说经典》（8卷）、《世界微型小说名家名作百年经典》（10卷）；电子版图书如《小小说的盛宴书系：别人的女郎》《诺贝尔文学奖获奖作家微型小说精选》等；网上资源如读秀、百链期刊、龙源期刊网等。

此外，众所周知，微型小说历来是中考、高考、四六级的语文和英语考试的听力、阅读理解、翻译、作文的模拟试题和真题材料。微型小说还是影视短剧、喜剧、小品的改编材料。

当然，还有社会影响。第一，多次荣获国家级奖项。1998年《爱旅无涯》获《中国青年报·青年参考》最受读者喜爱的翻译文学作品，2010年当选小小说存档作家，2002年"英汉经典阅读"系列获上海外国语大学学术文化节科研成果奖，2002年当选当代微型小说百家，2002年《译作》当选全国第四次微型小说续写大赛竞赛原作。第二，受到知名评论家张锦贻、陈勇等关注和评论达10余次。第三，曾受邀参加中央电视台、内蒙古电视台及电台、中国作家网的人物专访。第四，个人传记入选美国与捷克出版的《华文微型小说微自传》《中国当代微型小说百家论续集》《世界微型小说百家传论》。第五，因为翻译而收到来自世界各地、各行各业的读者来信、电话、邮件不计其数。

虽然近年我转向长篇小说的翻译，并以《老人与海》《房龙地理》《鹿出没》等再次获得读者的青睐，然而对于我来说，那些年，绞尽脑汁一字一句地写在稿纸上，满怀希冀地一封一封地把译稿投进邮筒，忐忑不安地在报亭、邮局一本一本地翻找自己的译作，欢天喜地买几本回家，进门就问女儿"Can you guess？"等她的固定答案"妈妈又发了！"都是我生命中一个一个的定格瞬间。微型小说翻译是我的"初心",而唯有"初心"是不能辜负的。因此,我于2015年开办了以我的微型小说翻译为内容的自媒体——微信公众号"白桦译林",收获了大量读者和转载,更促成了"译趣坊·世界微型小说精选"系列的陆续出版。

谨以此书感谢多年来扶持过我的报刊编辑老师,以及多年来一直乐于阅读我的微型小说的读者和学生。

目 录

content

一条毛毯 / The Blanket · 1

谁给了我耳朵 / Who Gave Me the Ears · 8

别人与母亲 / Mothers and Others · 12

心若在 / Will Power · 16

母亲写给世界的信 / A Special Letter · 20

我离家出走的那一天 / The Day I Ran Away from Home · 24

妈妈的电话 / Mom's Call · 31

生命中一直在等待的那一天 / A Legend of Love · 35

奇迹值多少钱 / How Much does a Miracle Cost · 45

熊孩子 / A Troublesome Child · 51

圣诞节快乐 / Happy Christmas · 53

我是你的 BF/ Do You Know What BF Means · 55

天作之合 / Made in Heaven · 59

冬夜 / A Winter Night · 73

爱上老师 / A Bouquet for Miss Benson · 78

所谓成长，无非是所见即所得 / Children Learn What They Live · 86

生活 / Life · 90

玫瑰之约 / The Red Rose · 92

银象胸针 / The Silver Elephant · 99

生死相随 / Life Together · 110

一封神奇的情书 / An Ingenious Letter · 117

有情人 / Letter in the Wallet · 121

天使何所似 / What do Angels Look Like · 132

现在是春天 / It's Spring · 135

爱情永不失明 / A Gift of Love · 137

情路崎岖 / Detour to Romance · 144

分文不取 / No Charge · 151

窗外 / A Room with a View · 155

失败意味着什么 / What does Failure Mean · 159

加利福尼亚的传说 / The Californian's Tale · 165

浮生半日 / Half a Day · 176

写给在天堂的妻子的信 / A Letter to His Wife in Paradise · 183

一条毛毯

弗罗伊德·戴尔

彼得不相信爸爸真的会做这件事——把爷爷送走。"走",他们就是这么说的,直到现在彼得都不相信这出自父亲的口。

可是,给爷爷买的毛毯就放在这里,明早爷爷就得离开,这是彼得和爷爷在一起的最后一个晚上了。爸爸去见那个他要迎娶的女孩了,要到很晚才能回来,所以,彼得和爷爷要晚点儿睡,说说话。

这是一个晴朗的九月的夜晚,银色的月亮高高地挂在天空上。洗完碗碟,爷孙搬出椅子走出屋子,坐在月光下。"我去拿口琴来给你吹几支老曲子。"爷爷说。

一会儿,爷爷从屋里出来了,拿来的不是口琴,而是那条黑红条纹的双人大毛毯。

"嗯,这毛毯多好啊!"老人轻轻地抚摸着膝头的毛毯说,"你爸真是孝顺啊,给我这老家伙带这么高级的毛毯走。你看这毛,一定很贵的,这么好的毛毯不会有几条。"

爷爷总这么说,他是为了避免难堪,他一直装着很想去政府办的养老院——那幢砖砌的大楼的样子,想象着,去那个地方与那么多老人一起共度晚年,拥有最好的一切……可彼得从没想到爸爸真会把爷爷送走，直到今晚看到爸爸带回这条毛毯。

"是条好毛毯。"彼得搭讪着走进小屋。他不是个爱哭鼻子的孩子，况且，他早已过了好哭鼻子的年龄了。他是进屋给爷爷拿口琴的。

爷爷站起来接口琴的时候毛毯滑落到地板上。爷爷吹了一会儿，然后说道，"你会记住这支曲子的。"

彼得呆呆地坐着，望着外面的溪谷。爸爸要迎娶那个姑娘了。是的，那个姑娘亲过彼得了，对彼得百般宠爱，还发誓说要做个好后妈什么的……

爷爷突然停下来，说道，"你爸要娶的姑娘不错。有个这么漂亮的妻子他会感觉又有了第二春。我这样的老头又何必在这碍事呢？我老了，七病八痛的，招人嫌呢。不，不！还是走为上策呀！好，再吹两支曲子我们就上床睡觉，我明天早晨再收拾毛毯。"

他们没有听到有两个人正沿着小路走来，爸爸拥着那个姑娘，姑娘容光焕发，脸蛋儿好像瓷娃娃。直到走进门廊，爷孙俩才听到她的笑声，琴声戛然而止。爸爸一声没吭，姑娘走到爷爷跟前得体地说道："明天早晨不能来送您，我现在来跟您告别的。"

"谢谢了，"爷爷眼睛低垂着说道。接着，爷爷看到了脚边的毛毯，弯腰拾了起来，"你看，"爷爷说道，"这是儿子送我的离别礼物。多好的毛毯！"

"是不错。"她摸了一下毛毯，"好高级呀！"她惊讶地重复道，"我得承认——这确实是一条高级毛毯！"她转向爸爸，冷冷地说，"一定花了不少钱吧？"

爸爸清了清嗓子，说道，"我想给他一条最好的……"

"还是双人的呢。"姑娘说道，似乎是在责备爸爸。

"是的，"老人说，"是条双人毛毯。一条一个老家伙即将带走的毛毯。"

彼得突然转身跑进了屋。他听到那姑娘还在责备爸爸，她回过味儿来了，这条毛毯花费了爸爸——她多少钱，都花在这条毛毯上了。爸爸开始慢慢动怒，姑娘突然怒气冲冲地拔腿就走了……

彼得出屋时她正回头冲爸爸喊，"解释也没用，他根本用不着双人毛毯。"她沿着那条小路跑了。

爸爸看着她，好像是不知所措的样子。

"哦，她说得对，"彼得说，"爸爸，给！"——彼得递给爸爸一把剪刀，"把毛毯剪成两块。"

爷爷和爸爸都盯着彼得看。"爸爸，我跟你说，把毛毯剪成两块，留下一块。"

"好主意，"爷爷温和地说，"我用不着这么大的毛毯。"

"是的，"彼得厉声说道，"老人家送走时给条单人毛毯就不错了。我们还能留下一半，以后迟早总有用处。"

"你这是什么意思？"爸爸问。

"我是说，"彼得慢腾腾地说，"等你老了，我送你走时给你这一半。"

大家都沉默了。好半天，爸爸走到爷爷面前呆呆地站着，没有一句话。爷爷把手放到他儿子的肩上低声说道："没关系，孩子，我知道你不是这么想的……"这时，彼得哭了。

但没什么，因为爷爷、爸爸都哭了……

The Blanket

By Floyd Dell

Peter hadn't really believed that Dad would be doing it—sending Granddad away. "Away" was what they were calling it. Not until now could he believe it of his father.

But here was the blanket that Dad had bought for Granddad, and in the morning he'd be going away. This was the last evening they'd be having together. Dad was off seeing that girl he was to marry. He would not be back till late, so Peter and Granddad could sit up and talk.

It was a fine September night, with a silver moon riding high. They washed up the supper dishes and then took their chairs out onto the porch. "I'll get my fiddle," said the old man, "and play you some of the old tunes."

But instead of the fiddle he brought out the blanket. It was a big double blanket, red with black stripes.

"Now, isn't that a fine blanket!" said the old man, smoothing it over his knees. "And isn't your father a kind man to be giving the old fellow a blanket like that to go away with? It cost something, it did—look at the wool of it! There'll be few blankets there the equal of this one!"

It was like Granddad to be saying that. He was trying to make it easier. He had pretended all along that he wanted to go away to the great brick building—the government place. There he'd be with so many other old fellows, having the best of everything... But Peter hadn't believed Dad would really do it, not until this night when he brought home the blanket.

"Oh, yes, it's a fine blanket," said Peter. He got up and went into the house. He wasn't the kind to cry and, besides, he was too old for that. He'd just gone in to fetch Granddad's fiddle.

The blanket slid to the floor as the old man took the fiddle and stood up. He tuned up for a minute, and then said, "This is one you'll like to remember."

Peter sat and looked out over the gully. Dad would marry that girl. Yes, that girl who had kissed Peter and fussed over him, saying she'd try to be a good mother to him, and all...

The tune stopped suddenly. Granddad said, "It's a fine girl your father's going to marry. He'll be feeling young again with a pretty wife like that. And what would an old fellow like me be doing around their house, getting in the way? An old nuisance, what with my talks of aches and pains. It's best that I go away, like I'm doing. One more tune or two, and then we'll be going to sleep. I'll pack up my blanket in the morning."

They didn't hear the two people coming down the path. Dad had one arm around the girl, whose bright face was like a doll's. But they heard her when she laughed, right close by the porch. Dad didn't say anything, but the girl came forward and spoke to Granddad prettily: "I won't be here when you leave in the morning, so I came over to say good-bye."

"It's kind of you," said Granddad, with his eyes cast down. Then, seeing the blanket at his feet, he stooped to pick it up. "And will you look at this," he said. "The fine blanket my son has given me to go away with."

"Yes," she said. "It's a fine blanket." She felt the wool and repeated in surprise, "A fine blanket—I'll say it is!" She turned to Dad and said to him coldly, "That blanket really cost something."

Dad cleared his throat and said, "I wanted him to have the best…"

"It's double, too," she said, as if accusing Dad.

"Yes," said Granddad, "it's double—a fine blanket for an old fellow to be going away with."

The boy went suddenly into the house. He was looking for something. He could hear that girl scolding Dad. She realized how much of Dad's money—her money, really—had gone for the blanket. Dad became angry in his slow way. And now she was suddenly going away in a huff...

As Peter came out, she turned and called back, "All the same, he doesn't need a double blanket!" And she ran off up the path.

Dad was looking after her as if he wasn't sure what he ought to do.

"Oh, she's right," Peter said. "Here, Dad!" —and he held out a pair of scissors. "Cut the blanket in two."

Both of them stared at the boy, startled. "Cut it in two, I tell you, Dad!" he cried out. "And keep the other half."

"That's not a bad idea," said Granddad gently. "I don't need so much of a blanket."

"Yes," the boy said harshly, "a single blanket's enough for an old man when he's sent away. We'll save the other half, Dad. It'll come in handy later."

"Now what do you mean by that?" asked Dad.

"I mean," said the boy slowly, "that I'll give it to you, Dad—when you're old and I'm sending you—away."

There was a silence. Then Dad went over to Granddad and stood before him, not speaking. But Granddad understood. He put out a hand and laid it on Dad's shoulder. And he heard Granddad whisper, "It's all right, son. I knew you didn't mean it..." And then Peter cried.

But it didn't matter—because they were all crying together.

谁给了我耳朵

"我可以看看我的宝宝吗？"初为人母的她开心地问道。

当裹着的婴儿放到她臂弯里，她掀开裹着婴儿的布，在看到他的小脸时，不由地倒吸了一口气。医生快速地转过身，透过医院的高高的窗户向外看去。婴儿生下来就没有耳朵。

时间证明，婴儿虽然没长耳朵，听力却完全没有问题，只是有损他的形象。一天，当他匆匆从学校跑回家，扑进母亲的怀里时，她幽幽长叹，意识到他的生命历程中注定会有一连串的伤心。

他将遭到的不幸脱口而出："一个男孩，一个大个子男孩……他叫我怪胎。"

他已经长大了，虽然不幸没有了耳朵，长得还是挺帅的，同学们很喜欢他，若不是因为没有耳朵，他很可能都能当上班长。他对文学和音乐很有天赋，后天发展得也很好。

"可是你可以跟其他年轻人一样的。"母亲责备道，却是语重心长的。

男孩的父亲与家庭医生商量……"难道就无计可施了吗？"

"如果能够找到的话，我认为可以移植一双外耳。"医生做了决定，于是他们开始寻求一个愿意为这个年轻人做出牺牲的人。

两年过去了。父亲对儿子说道，"孩子，你要住院了。我和你妈找到愿意为你捐献耳朵的人了，不过捐献人要求保密。"

手术获得了巨大成功，一个新人诞生了。他的潜能得到充分发展，在中学和大学都取得了一系列的成功。

后来，他结了婚，进入外交部门。一天，他问父亲："可是我一定要知道，是谁给我捐献的耳朵？谁给予了我这么多？我永远都无法报答他的恩情。"

"我也认为你无法报答，"父亲说，"但是协议上说不让你知道……还不到时候。"

数年来，他们严格保守着这个埋藏得很深的秘密，但是真相大白这一天终于还是来了，这也是儿子度过的最黑暗的日子。他和父亲站在母亲的棺材前，父亲慢慢地、轻柔地，向前伸出一只手，掀开母亲浓密的、红褐色的头发：母亲竟然没有外耳！

"你母亲说过她很高兴，她从不理发，"父亲轻柔地低声说，"但没人觉得母亲不如以前美丽，是吧？"

Who Gave Me the Ears

"Can I see my baby?" the happy new mother asked.

When the bundle was nestled in her arms and she moved the fold of cloth to look upon his tiny face, she gasped. The doctor turned quickly and looked out the tall hospital window. The baby had been born without ears.

Time proved that the baby's hearing was perfect. It was only his appearance that was marred. When he rushed home from school one day and flung himself into his mother's arms, she sighed, knowing that his life was to be a succession of heartbreaks.

He blurted out the tragedy. "A boy, a big boy…called me a freak."

He grew up, handsome except for his misfortune. A favorite with his fellow students, he might have been class president, but for that. He developed a gift, a talent for literature and music.

"But you might mingle with other young people," his mother reproved him, but felt a kindness in her heart.

The boy's father had a session with the family physician… "Could nothing be done?"

"I believe I could graft on a pair of outer ears, if they could be procured," the doctor decided. So the search began for a person who would make such a sacrifice for a young man.

Two years went by. Then, "You're going to the hospital, son. Mother and I have someone who will donate the ears you need. But it's a secret." said the father.

The operation was a brilliant success, and a new person emerged. His talents blossomed into genius, and school and college became a series of triumphs.

Later he married and entered the diplomatic service. "But I must know," he asked his father, "Who gave me the ears? Who gave me so much? I could never do enough for him."

"I do not believe you could," said the father, "but the agreement was that you are not to know…not yet."

The years kept their profound secret, but the day did come. One of the darkest days that ever passed through a son. He stood with his father over his mother's casket. Slowly, tenderly, the father stretched forth a hand and raised the thick, reddish brown hair to reveal that the mother had no outer ears.

"Mother said she was glad she never let her hair be cut," his father whispered gently, "and nobody ever thought mother less beautiful, did they?"

别人与母亲

A. R. 韦尔斯

我们吵闹，别人避之不及心生厌，
母亲爱子嬉戏乐相伴。

我们摔倒，别人责骂响耳畔，
母亲以吻止泪暖心田。

别人工作全凭耐心一片，
母亲日夜操劳不知疲倦。

别人的爱忽多忽少，
母亲的爱有增无减。

别人的原谅尚留怨，
母亲的宽恕到永远。

别人翻旧账报宿怨，

母亲的账清零金不换。

别人对我们疑神疑鬼,
母亲对我们的笃信未曾断。

别人的信仰弃之敝屣,
母亲的祷告一遍又一遍。

Mothers and Others

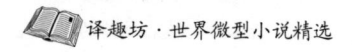

By A. R. Wells

Others weary of the noise,
Mothers play with girls and boys.

Others scold because we fell,
Mother's kiss and make it well.

Others work with patient will,
Mothers labor later still.

Others' love is more or less,
Mothers love with steadiness.

Others pardon, hating yet,
Mothers pardon and forget.

Others keep the ancient score,

Mothers never shut the door.

Others grow incredulous,
Mothers still believe in us.

Others throw their faith away,
Mothers pray, and pray, and pray.

心若在

有一个老人住在明尼苏达州,他想把自己土豆园的地翻一翻,可是却很困难,因为能帮上他忙的独生子,此时却在监狱服刑。老人给监狱里的儿子写信提到了这个情况。

亲爱的儿子,

一想到今年不能种土豆了,我就感觉很不好。我不愿意错过翻地时间,因为你妈妈一直喜欢播种时节。我年老体弱,翻不动地了,要是你在的话,我的麻烦就没有了,我知道,你现在要是不在监狱的话,你会给我翻地的。

爱你的,

爸爸

很快,老人就接到了一封电报:"爸爸,看在上帝的分儿上,不要挖菜园!我把枪埋在菜园里啦!"

次日清晨,十二个联邦调查局的特工和当地警察局的官员出现了,他们把整个菜园的地翻了个遍,也没有找到枪支。

老人大感不解,于是给儿子又写了封短信,告诉儿子所发生的一切,问儿子下一步怎么办。

他儿子的回答是:"去种你的土豆吧,爸爸。我在这里能为你做的也就只有这些了。"

不论你在天涯海角,只要你下定决心要做内心最想做的事,你就一定可以做得到。重要的是你的心怎么想,而非你是什么身份或者身在何方。

Will Power

An old man lived alone in Minnesota. He wanted to spade his potato garden, but it was very hard. His only son, who would have helped him, was in prison. The old man wrote a letter to his son and mentioned his situation.

Dear son,

I am feeling pretty bad because it seems I won't be able to plant my potato garden this year. I hate to miss doing the garden, because your mother always loved planting time. I'm just getting too old to be digging up a garden plot. If you were here, all my troubles would be over. I know you would dig the plot for me, if you weren't in prison.

Love,

Dad

Shortly, the old man received a telegram: "For Heaven's sake, Dad, don't dig up the garden! That's where I buried the GUNS!"

The next morning, a dozen FBI agents and local police officers showed up and dug up the entire garden without finding any guns.

Confused, the old man wrote another note to his son telling him what happened, and asked him what to do next.

His son's reply was: "Go ahead and plant your potatoes, Dad. It's the best I could do for you from here."

No matter where you are in the world, if you have decided to do something deep from you heart, you can do it. It is the thought that matters, not where you are or where the person is.

母亲写给世界的信

亲爱的世界:

我的儿子今天就要开始上学读书了。

一时之间,他会感觉陌生而又新鲜。我希望你能够对他温柔一些。

你也是知道的,到现在为止,他一直是家中的小皇帝。

一直是后院的大王。

我一直与他寸步不离,忙着为他治疗伤口,抚慰他的种种情绪。

而现在——一切都将截然不同了。

今天清晨,他就要走下前门的楼梯,冲我挥手,然后开始他的伟大的历险,这一历险可能包括战争、悲剧和痛苦。

既然活在这个世上,他就需要信念、爱心和勇气。

所以,世界啊,我希望你能够时不时握住他稚嫩的小手,教会他应当掌握的种种本领。

教育他吧——可是,如果可能的话,温柔一些。

教他知道,恶棍出现的地方,必有英雄同在;奸诈的政客出现的地方,必有献身义士同在;敌人出现的地方,必有朋友同在。

教他感受书籍的神奇魅力。

给他时间,让他静思大自然永恒的奥秘:空中的飞鸟,阳光里的蜜蜂,青山上的繁花。

教给他,失败远比欺骗光荣。

教他对自己的信念坚信不疑,哪怕大家都说是错的。

教他可以最高价出售自己的体力和脑力,但绝不可出卖良心和灵魂。

教他对众生喧哗置若罔闻……并在自己确信该出手时挺身而出。

温柔地教导他吧,世界,但是不要溺爱他,因为烈火出好钢。

这是一个大单,世界,但是请你竭尽全力。

他是一个这么可爱的小家伙。

A Special Letter

Dear World,

 My son starts school today.

 It's going to be strange and new to him for a while, and I wish you would sort of treat him gently.

 You see, up to now, he's been king of the roost.

 He's been boss of the backyard.

 I have always been around to repair his wounds, and to soothe his feelings.

 But now—things are going to be different.

 This morning, he's going to walk down the front steps, wave his hand and start on his great adventure that will probably include wars and tragedy and sorrow.

 To live his life in the world he has to live in will require faith and love and courage.

 So, World, I wish you would sort of take him by his young hand and teach him the things he will have to know.

 Teach him—but gently, if you can.

 Teach him that for every scoundrel there is a hero; that for every crooked politician there is a dedicated leader; that for every enemy there is a friend.

Teach him the wonders of books.

Give him quiet time to ponder the eternal mystery of birds in the sky, bees in the sun, and flowers on the green hill.

Teach him it is far more honorable to fail than to cheat.

Teach him to have faith in his own ideas, even if everyone tells him they are wrong.

Teach him to sell his brawn and brains to the highest bidder, but never to put a price on his heart and soul.

Teach him to close his ears to a howling mob...and to stand and fight if he thinks he's right.

Teach him gently, World, but don't coddle him, because only the test of fire makes fine steel.

This is a big order, World, but see what you can do.

He's such a nice little fellow.

我离家出走的那一天

黛尔·艾伦·肖克利

我站在大门口,望着外面湿漉漉、冷冰冰的草坪。那几周的日子也是沉闷乏味的。头顶上,灰色的天空低垂着。那棵大橡树,树皮剥落,弯曲的手指指向苍穹,仿佛在祈求太阳赐予温暖。我也有同感。太阳是否还会再次照耀大地?

我不知道我是着了什么魔,但是在那一刻,我特别渴望离家出走,去一个有阳光有大海的具有异国情调的地方,那里没有人知道我的名字,风吹过我的头发,雨伞只是用来遮阳的。

你有没有想过,独自一人驱车前往未知的地方,到一个你不需要处理那些似乎永远都解决不了的棘手问题的地方,哪怕只是一瞬间?

当时我确实离家出走了,当时我的点滴的想法正是这样。

那天晚上很晚的时候。我不记得当时是为什么了,但我和丈夫大吵特吵了一顿,我们俩都说了些彼此本来并不想说的话,最后,我说:"我要走了。"他说:"好。越快越好。"

我把几件东西扔在一个小手提箱里,"砰"的一声关上了门,根本不知道我要去哪里。在兜了几分钟的圈子以后,我在当地的杂货店停下来,买了一些我忘了带的东西,匆匆忙忙地出了店门。

但还没等我走下第一个通道,我的手机就响了。原来是已经长大成人的女儿打来的。我接了电话,她问道:"嘿,妈妈。你在哪里?"

我立刻明白她已经知道真相了,她声音中的某种东西泄露了秘密。

"嘿,亲爱的。我出去玩一会儿。怎么了?"

"嗯,你在哪儿?"坚持是她的名字。

"刚刚出去。怎么啦?"

"妈妈,爸爸很担心你。"

"他怎么会为我担心呢?我才出去二十分钟。他给你打电话了吗?"我很不安。

"没有,他没有给我打电话。我打电话来找你说话,是的,他真的很担心你。"

"嗯,他应该早就料到的,"我说,想起了他口无遮拦出口伤人的话,我的火儿又上来了。"听着,亲爱的。我真的需要挂断电话。你可以告诉你爸爸我很好。我很好。我爱你,明天我给你打电话。"

我挂断电话,在商店里徘徊,想把我的思绪整理一下。我有钱,所以我决定去附近的旅馆,试着睡一会儿。上帝知道我有多需要睡眠。

我给买的东西付钱的时候,比我平时单独外出的时间要晚得多。这次我把车停在离商店很近的地方,所以实际上是一路小跑回到的车里。一上车,我就锁上车门,发动了车子。我没有看车外面。车的雨刷下别了一张大大的方形白纸。那到底是什么东西?

当我的眼睛渐渐适应了眼前的黑暗以后,雨刷上的一切变得清晰了。在一张白纸上,用一个黑色的记号笔画了一个大大的心,心里写着这些话:"求求你回家吧!!我想念你!我爱你!"

还没等我看完,一辆卡车就在我旁边停了下来。从车窗里探出头来的不是别人,正是我的丈夫。显然,他已经叫来了搜索队。我的女儿坐在他旁边，咧着嘴笑着。

这时，我也笑了起来。我笑得那么厉害，几乎喜极而泣。尽管我竭尽全力要离家出走，这个爱我的野人和笨蛋却竭尽全力地追踪我。有他坐在那里，瞪着小狗似的眼睛，我现在是不可能那么顺利地离开了。

当我跟着他出停车场时，我意识到我们刚才的行为是多么愚蠢，为鸡毛蒜皮的事情争吵，而我又是多么幸运，我最爱的那个人爱我，会来找我，还找到了我，带我回家。

The Day I Ran Away from Home

By Dayle Allen Shockley

I stood at the front door, looking out over the cold wet lawn. It had been a soggy couple of weeks. Overhead, the sky hung low and gray. The big oak, stripped barren, pointed crooked fingers toward the heavens as if pleading for the sun's warmth. I echoed that sentiment. Would the sun ever shine again?

I don't know what came over me, but in that moment, I longed to run away from home, to an exotic place filled with sunshine and sea, where no one knew my name, where the wind blew through my hair, and umbrellas were used only for shade.

Have you ever wished, even for a split second, to drive off to places unknown, alone? To a place where you don't have to deal with the same old issues that keep turning up through the years, seemingly never to be resolved?

There was that time I actually did run away, sort of. The details went something like this.

It was late one evening. I don't recall what it was about, but

The Man and I had a very big and ugly argument. We both said things we didn't mean and, in the end, I said, "I'm leaving," and he said, "Good. The sooner, the better."

I threw a few things in a small suitcase and slammed the door behind me, not having a clue where I was going. After driving in circles for several minutes, I stopped at my local grocery to pick up some personal items I'd forgotten to pack in my heated rush to get out of the house.

But before I got down the first aisle, my cell phone rang. It was my grown daughter calling. I answered the phone and she said, "Hey, Mom. Where are you?"

Instantly, I knew she knew. Something in her voice gave it away.

"Hey, sweetie. I'm out for a bit. What's up?"

"Well, where are you?" Persistence is her middle name.

"Just out. Why?"

"Mom, Dad is worried about you."

"How can he be worried about me? I've been gone a total of twenty minutes. Did he call you?" I was perturbed.

"No, he didn't call me. I called and asked to talk to you and yes, he is really worried about you."

"Well, he should have thought of that sooner," I said, my anger returning, remembering all of the hateful things he'd spouted. "Listen, sweetie. I really need to get off the phone. You can tell your dad that I'm fine. I'm just fine. I love you, and I'll call you tomorrow."

I hung up and lingered in the store, trying to get my thoughts together. I had money, so I decided I'd go to a nearby hotel and attempt to get some sleep. Lord knew I needed it.

By the time I paid for my purchases, it was much later than I liked to be out alone. I'd parked a good distance from the store and practically ran to my car. Once inside, I locked the doors, cranked the engine, and started to drive off. But I couldn't see out. A large square of white paper was stuck under my windshield wiper. What on earth?

As my eyes adjusted to the dark, it became clear. There, on a white piece of copy paper, drawn with a black marker, was a big heart encircling these words: "Please come home!! I miss you! I love you!"

Before I could process it all, a truck pulled up alongside me. Hanging out the window was none other than my husband. Apparently, he'd called out the search party. Beside him, grinning from ear-to-ear, sat my daughter.

And that's when I started laughing. I laughed so hard I cried. Despite my best efforts to run away from home, the wild and zany man who loved me had managed to track me down. I couldn't very well leave now, not with him sitting there with puppy-dog eyes.

As I followed him out of the parking lot, I realized how foolish we'd been, arguing over insignificant things, and how blessed I was that the man I loved most in the world loved me back and had come looking for me and found me, and was leading me home again.

妈妈的电话

黎明时分,电话铃声响起。我前夜宿醉,正在昏昏欲睡,接起电话,听到妈妈的声音:"汤米,快起床!今天要开会。"

我看看手表,便不高兴地叫起来:"我不是说六点整再叫我吗?我还想多睡一会儿,现在都被你吵醒了!"

妈妈在那头沉默不语,我随即切断了电话。

我冒着倾盆大雨,急急忙忙赶车上班。在车站等公车的时候,我旁边站着一对白发苍苍的老夫妇,我听见老头对老太太嘟嘟囔囔道:"都是你的错,你看你,我一整晚都没睡好,你还那么早就催我,现在却要等这么长时间!"

公车终于来了,司机是一个年轻人。

我刚一上车,他就关上车门,我赶紧提醒他:"司机,后面还有两位老人,他们还没上车呀!"

年轻人却带着一脸灿烂的笑容答道:"哦,没关系,那是我爸妈!今天是我第一天到汽车公司上班,他们专程来照看我第一天顺利开工的。"

他回头向两个老人挥了挥手,就开动了车子。

看到这幅景象,我立刻想起妈妈早上的电话,一种挥之不去的愧疚感涌上了我的心头。

那天下班以后,我给妈妈打电话,没想到我还没道歉,妈妈就先说:"嗨,孩子,早上那么早叫你,都是我不好,因为担心你开会迟到,我一晚上没有睡好……"

Mom's Call

The phone ring sounded at cockcrow, disturbing me from my sleepy hangover with Mom's words, "Tommy, time to get up! You'll have a meeting today."

I checked it up at my wrist watch and cried with a grouch, "Didn't tell you to call at six sharp? I do need more sleep, but now it is you who messed it up!"

Mom remained silent for quite a while before I rang off.

I hurried out to catch the bus to work against a heavy rain. I stood at the bus stop with a couple of gray-haired husband and wife standing by my side when the old man grumbled to his old lady, "It is all your fault, you know, I didn't have a good sleep the whole night. You woke me up at such an early hour and we have to wait so long!"

Here came the bus and it was a young driver.

No sooner had I got onto the bus than the door was closed. At this, I gave the driver an immediate reminder, "Hi, why not let the two elderly persons get on the bus?"

The young lad said with a big smile, "Oh, never mind! They

are my old guys! Today is the first day I get a foot in the door of the bus company and they come over all the way from home to see whether I can start off on the right foot at work."

He looked back, waving to the two elderly persons, and drove the bus off.

It was not until I saw all this that I immediately thought of my Mom's call in early morning and a lingering sense of guilt crept over me.

When I got back from work, I called Mom to say sorry, but to my surprise, Mom said, "Hi, Honey! It is me to blame to have called you at such an early hour. As I was worried that you might be late for the meeting, I didn't sleep well…"

生命中一直在等待的那一天

爱德华·威尔曼就要辞别家人和古老乡村，去美国寻求更好的生活了。爸爸把家里所有的积蓄藏在一个皮包里，把皮包交给了他。"这里日子快过不下去了，"爸爸拥抱着儿子，跟他道别，叮嘱道，"你可是咱们全家的希望啊！"

爱德华搭上了一艘大西洋货船，货船专门为愿意无偿为货船铲煤的年轻人提供一个月的免费旅行。如果爱德华能够在美国科罗拉多州的落基山脉淘到黄金，那么，他的家人最终就能够到美国跟他团聚了。

几个月过去了，爱德华不知疲倦地工作，他找到了一个小的金矿矿脉，给他带来了一些微薄却很稳定的收入。一天下来，当他走进他那有两个房间的小木屋的时候，他多么希望他钟爱的女人能在家里迎接他的归来啊！直到如今，他唯一感到遗憾的是他在前来美国冒险之前没有正式向英格里德求婚。他家和英格里德家是多年的世交，至少从他记事儿起就是。她那一头长长的、飘逸的秀发，她那灿烂的微笑，使得她成为汉德森姐妹中最漂亮的一个，他一直都默默地爱着英格里德，期盼着有朝一日能够娶她为妻。记得他在教堂野餐时，他也是从一开始就坐在她的身边，还总是找一些愚蠢的理由去她家，只是为了见她一面。现在，每天晚上在小木屋里临睡之前，他总是渴望能够轻抚着英格里德的长发，把她拥入怀中。最后，他提笔给他的爸爸写了一封信，求他帮助他梦想成真。

近一年以后，终于，一封电报发了过来，上面写着令他的人生完满的计划。汉德森先生已经同意让他的女儿到美国来了。由于她很有商业头脑，而且又能吃苦耐劳，所以，她将在爱德华的身边工作一年，帮助他打理金矿的事务，促进金矿生意发展。到那时，他们两家就可以一起来美国参加他们的婚礼了。

爱德华快乐得心都飞翔起来。在接下来的一个月里，他竭尽全力把小木屋改造成一个"家"的样子。他买了一张轻便小床，放在起居室里留自己睡觉，而把他原来的卧室改造得适合女人居住。他用从面粉袋子上剪下来的花布做成窗帘，换下了原来挂在肮脏不堪的窗户上的粗麻布口袋。他还从牧场里采摘来干的山艾，插在锡罐里，摆在床头柜上。

终于，他生命里一直在等待的那一天来了。他手捧着新采来的一束雏菊，前往火车站迎接心上人的到来。当火车喷着蒸汽，车轮发出刺耳的尖叫声徐徐驶进车站的时候，爱德华翘首向每一扇车窗里张望着，期待着能见到英格里德那长长的秀发和灿烂的笑容。

由于热切的期待，他的心在剧烈地跳动着，接着，他的心却重重地沉了下来，因为，走下火车的不是英格里德，而是她的姐姐玛塔。她羞答答地站在他面前，眼睛注视着地面。

爱德华目瞪口呆地站在那里。过了一会儿，他才颤抖着手把花束递给了玛塔。"欢迎，"他轻声说道，眼睛仿佛被灼烧一样难受。这时，玛塔那其貌不扬的脸上露出了一丝微笑。

"当爸爸告诉我说你希望我能来美国的时候，我很高兴。"玛塔飞快地与他的眼睛对视了一下，就又垂下了头。

"我来替你拿行李吧。"爱德华勉强挤出一丝笑容说。然后,他们一起向马车走去。

果然不出汉德森先生和爸爸的预料,玛塔确实具有很强的商业头脑。当爱德华在金矿工作的时候,她则在办公室里打理各方面的事务。她在起居室的一个角落里,临时找了一张桌子当办公桌,并把所有顾客提出的要求的成本核算都详细记录了下来。在半年的时间里,他们的资产就翻了一番。

她还会做美味可口的饭菜,她的微笑是那么恬静,这一切都给他的小木屋平添了一丝美好的女人的气息。可是,她却不是他想要的女人,每天晚上,当他拖着疲惫不堪的身体倒在他的轻便小床上时,他总是会感到深深的遗憾。他们为什么让玛塔来?他是不是再也见不到英格里德了?他要娶英格里德为妻的终生梦想是不是被遗忘了?

就这样,一年过去了。在这一年里,玛塔和爱德华一起工作,一起玩乐,却不曾相爱。有一次,在回自己的房间之前,玛塔在爱德华的脸颊上轻轻地吻了一下。虽然,爱德华只是尴尬地笑了笑,然而,就是从那时起,他们之间的任何一次愉快的群山间远足,晚饭后坐在走廊里的长谈,似乎都让玛塔感到心满意足。

一个春日的午后,暴雨冲下山坡,把他们的金矿的入口冲垮了。爱德华手忙脚乱地把粗麻袋装满沙子堆在一起,企图阻挡住水流。他已经浑身湿透,筋疲力尽了,可是,他的努力似乎没有用处。就在这时,突然,玛塔出现在他的身边,打开了一个粗麻袋,爱德华用铁锹往粗麻袋装起了沙子。然后,玛塔竟像一个男人一样,把装满沙子的粗麻袋扔进那一堆装满沙子的粗麻袋上,接着,她又撑开了另一个粗麻布袋……他们一起在齐膝深的淤泥里奋战了好几个小时,直到雨停。

然后，他们手拉着手回到了小木屋。喝过一碗热汤之后，爱德华感慨地说："如果没有你，我根本保不住金矿。谢谢你，玛塔。"

"不用谢，"她答道，脸上依旧荡漾着恬静的微笑，一如既往，然后，她默默地走进自己的房间里。

几天之后，爱德华收到了一封电报，电报上说汉德森和威尔曼两家将于下星期抵达美国。尽管，爱德华竭力克制，但是，一想到又要见到英格里德，他的心又剧烈地跳动起来，一如既往。

爱德华和玛塔来到了火车站，他们看到了自己的家人走下火车，从月台那一头走来。英格里德出现了。这时，玛塔转过身来对爱德华说："去迎接她吧。"

爱德华惊讶地看着玛塔，结结巴巴地问："你是什么意思？"

"爱德华，其实我早就知道我并不是你所希望的来这里的那个汉德森家的女儿。我曾经看到过你和英格里德在教堂野餐时谈情说爱。"玛塔一边说着，一边向正走下火车踏板的妹妹点点头。

"我知道你想娶的人是她，不是我。"

"但是……"

"嘘——"玛塔把她的手指压在爱德华的嘴唇上，说："我确实爱你，爱德华，一直都爱。正因为如此，所以，我真诚地希望你能幸福。快去迎接她吧。"

爱德华一把抓住了玛塔压在他嘴唇上的手，紧紧地握着。玛塔抬起头，凝视着他。爱德华第一次发现玛塔竟是如此美丽！他回忆起他们在牧场上漫步，寂静的傍晚在篝火旁谈心，她跟他并肩作战装粗麻沙袋。此时此刻，爱德华才意识到了早在几个月以前就应该已经意识到的问题了。

"不,玛塔。我想要的人是你。"说着,爱德华将她拥入怀中。他那积聚在胸中的爱喷发出来,他亲吻着她。这时,他们的家人已经聚拢到了他们的身旁,齐声欢呼道:"哦,真是太好了,我们就是来参加婚礼的!"

A Legend of Love

Edward Wellman bade goodbye to his family in the old country headed for a better life in America. Papa handed him the family's savings hidden in a leather satchel. "Times are desperate here," he said, hugging his son goodbye. "You are our hope."

Edward boarded the Atlantic freighter offering free transport to young men willing to shovel coal in return for the month-long journey. If Edward struck gold in the Colorado Rockies, the rest of the family could eventually join him.

For months, Edward worked his claim tirelessly, and the small vein of gold provided a moderate but steady income. At the end of each day, as he walked through the door of his two-room cabin, he yearned for the woman he loved to greet him. Leaving Ingrid behind before he could officially court her had been his only regret in accepting this American adventure. Their families had been friends for years and for as long as he could remember, he had secretly hoped to make Ingrid his wife. Her long, flowing hair and radiant smile made her the most beautiful of the Henderson sisters. He had just begun sitting by her at church picnics and making up silly reasons to stop by her house, just so he could see her. As he went to sleep in his cabin each night, Edward longed to stroke her hair and hold her in his arms. Finally, he wrote to Papa, asking him to help make his dream come true.

After nearly a year, a telegraph came with a plan to make his life complete. Mr. Henderson had agreed to send his daughter to Edward in America. Because she was a hardworking young woman with a good mind for business, she would work alongside Edward for a year to help the mining business grow. By then both families could afford to come to America for their wedding.

Edward's heart soared with joy as he spent the next month trying to make the cabin into a home. He bought a cot for him to sleep on in the living area and tried to make his former bedroom suitable for a woman. Floral cloth from flour sacks replaced the burlap-bag curtains covering the dirty window. He arranged dried sage from the meadow into a tin can on the nightstand.

At last, the day he had been waiting for his whole life arrived. With a bouquet of fresh-picked daisies in hand, he left for the train depot. Steam billowed and wheels screeched as the train crawled to a stop. Edward scanned every window looking for Ingrid's glowing hair and smile.

His heart beat with eager anticipation, then stopped with a sinking thud. Not Ingrid, but her older sister Marta, stepped down from the train. She stood shyly before him, her eyes cast down.

Edward only stared dumbfounded. Then with shaking hands he offered Marta the bouquet. "Welcome," he whispered, his eyes burning. A smile etched across her plain face.

"I was pleased when Papa said you sent for me," Marta said, looking into his eyes briefly, before dropping her head again.

"I'll get your bags," Edward said with a fake smile. Together they headed for the buggy.

Mr. Henderson and Papa were right. Marta did have a great grasp of business. While Edward worked the mine, she worked the office. From her makeshift desk in one corner of the living area, she kept detailed records of all claim activity. Within six months, their assets doubled.

Her delicious meals and quiet smile graced the cabin with a wonderful woman's touch. But the wrong woman, Edward mourned as he collapsed onto his cot each night. Why did they send Marta? Would he ever see Ingrid again? Was his lifelong dream to have her as his wife forsaken?

For a year, Marta and Edward worked and played and laughed, but never loved. Once, Marta had kissed Edward on the cheek before retiring to her room. He only smiled awkwardly. From then on, she seemed content with their exhilarating hikes in the mountains and long talks on the porch after suppers.

One spring afternoon, torrential rains washed down the hillside, eroding the entrance to their mine. Furiously, Edward filled sand bags and stacked them in the water's path. Soaked and exhausted, his frantic efforts seemed futile. Suddenly there was Marta at his side holding the next burlap bag open. Edward shoveled sand inside, then with the strength of any man, Marta hurled it onto the pile and opened another bag... For hours they worked, knee-deep in mud, until the rains diminished.

Hand in hand, they walked back to the cabin. Over warm soup Edward sighed, "I never could have saved the mine without you. Thank you, Marta."

"You're welcome," she answered with her usual smile, then went quietly to her room.

A few days later, a telegraph came announcing the arrival of the Henderson and Wellman families next week. As much as he tried to stifle it, the thought of seeing Ingrid again started Edward's heart beating in the old familiar way.

Together, he and Marta went to the train station. They watched as their families exited the train at the far end of the platform. When Ingrid appeared, Marta turned to Edward. "Go to her," she said.

Astonished, Edward stammered, "What do you mean?"

"Edward, I have always known I was not the Henderson girl you intended to send for. I had watched you flirt with Ingrid at the church picnics." She nodded toward her sister descending the train steps.

"I know it is she, not me, you desire for your wife."

"But..."

Marta placed her fingers over his lips. "Shh," she hushed him. "I do love you, Edward. I always have. And because of that, all I really want is your happiness. Go to her."

He took her hand from his face and held it. As she gazed up at him, he saw for the first time how beautiful she was. He recalled their walks in the meadows, their quiet evenings before the fire, her working beside him with the sandbags. It was then he realized what he had known for months.

"No, Marta. It is you I want." Sweeping her into his arms, he kissed her with all the love bursting inside him. Their families gathered around them chorusing, "We are here for the wedding!"

奇迹值多少钱

苔丝八岁那年就已经很懂事了。有一天,她听见爸爸妈妈在说她弟弟安德鲁的事。她只听出弟弟病得很厉害,家里却根本拿不出钱来看病。爸爸已经付不起医药费和房子的月供了,他们下个月就得搬到公寓楼去住。

现在弟弟需要接受一个手术才有可能保住性命,可是手术费用高昂,看起来没有人会借钱给他们。她听见爸爸用绝望的口气,对泪流满面的母亲低声说道:"现在只有奇迹才能救得了他。"

苔丝走到自己的卧室,从壁橱里一个隐蔽的地方翻出一只玻璃果酱罐子。她把里面所有的零钱都倒出来摊在地板上,仔细地数起来。数了三遍结果都一样。总数一定要一样,不能出半点差错。她小心翼翼地把硬币放回罐子里,拧上盖子,然后溜出后门,向6个街区外的瑞克苏尔药店走去,那家店门上有一个很大的红色的印第安酋长标志。

她耐心地等着药剂师过来招呼,可是当时他太忙了。苔丝扭动双脚在地面上摩擦着,弄出很大的声响来,没人理她。她使劲儿用最招人厌烦的声音清了清嗓子,还是没用。

最后她从罐子里取出一枚二十五美分的硬币,猛地往玻璃柜台上一拍。这次奏效了。"你需要点什么?"药剂师恼火地问道,"我正跟我从芝加哥来的弟弟说话呢,我们已经有好长时间没见了。"他只是随口一问，并没有等苔丝回答他。

"嗯，我也正想跟你说说我弟弟的事呢，"苔丝也用同样恼火的语调回敬他，"他病得非常、非常厉害……所以我想买一个奇迹。"

"你说什么？"药剂师问。

"他的名字叫安德鲁，他的脑子里长了一个坏东西。爸爸说现在只有奇迹才能救得了他。那奇迹多少钱一个呢？"

"小姑娘，我们这儿没有奇迹卖，非常抱歉，我帮不了你。"药剂师说道，口气稍微柔和起来。

"你听我说，我付得起钱。要是不够的话，我再去拿。你就告诉我一个奇迹要多少钱嘛。"

那个药剂师的弟弟穿着非常体面。他弯下腰，问这个小姑娘："你弟弟需要一个什么样的奇迹呢？"

"我不知道，"苔丝的眼泪涌了出来，"我只知道他病得很厉害，妈妈说他需要动手术，可是爸爸拿不出钱，所以我想用自己的钱。"

"你带了多少钱呢？"那个从芝加哥来的人问道。

"一美元十一美分。"苔丝回答，声音低得几乎听不见，"我现在只有这么多，不过需要的话我还可以再去拿。"

"哇，真是太巧了，"那人微笑着说道，"一美元十一美分，给弟弟用的奇迹正好是这个价格。"

他一手接过钱，用另一只手抓起她戴着露指手套的手，说："带我去你家，我要看看你弟弟的情况，见见你父母。看看我这儿是不是有你需要的奇迹。"

那个穿着体面的人叫卡尔顿·阿姆斯特朗，是一位神经外科医生。他免费给安德鲁做了手术，没过多久安德鲁就痊愈回家了。事后，苔丝的父母开心地谈到过去，那一连串事情的发生才让他们有了今天。

"那天的手术,"她母亲低声说道,"的确是个奇迹,我真想知道值多少钱。"

苔丝笑了,她知道奇迹的准确价格是——一美元十一美分,再加上一个小孩儿执着的信念。

How Much does a Miracle Cost

Tess was a precocious eight-year-old girl when she heard her Mom and Dad talking about her little brother, Andrew. All she knew was that he was very sick and they were completely out of money. They were moving to an apartment complex next month because Daddy didn't have the money for the doctor's bills and our house.

Only a very costly surgery could save him now and it was looking like there was no-one to loan them the money. She heard Daddy say to her tearful Mother with whispered desperation, "Only a miracle can save him now."

Tess went to her bedroom and pulled a glass jelly jar from its hiding place in the closet. She poured all the change out on the floor and counted it carefully. Three times, even. The total had to be exactly perfect. No chance here for mistakes. Carefully placing the coins back in the jar and twisting on the cap, she slipped out the back door and made her way 6 blocks to Rexall's Drug Store with the big red Indian Chief sign above the door.

She waited patiently for the pharmacist to give her some

attention but he was too busy at this moment. Tess twisted her feet to make a noise. Nothing. She cleared her throat with the most disgusting sound she could muster. No good.

Finally she took a quarter from her jar and banged it on the glass counter. That did it! "And what do you want?" The pharmacist asked in an annoyed tone of voice. "I'm talking to my brother from Chicago whom I haven't seen in ages," he said without waiting for a reply to his question.

"Well, I want to talk to you about my brother," Tess answered back in the same annoyed tone. "He's really, really sick...and I want to buy a miracle."

"I beg your pardon?" said the pharmacist.

"His name is Andrew and he has something bad growing inside his head and my Daddy says only a miracle can save him now. So how much does a miracle cost?"

"We don't sell miracles here, little girl. I'm sorry but I can't help you." the pharmacist said, softening a little.

"Listen, I have the money to pay for it. If it isn't enough, I will get the rest. Just tell me how much it costs."

The pharmacist's brother was a well-dressed man. He stooped down and asked the little girl, "What kind of a miracle does your brother need?"

"I don't know," Tess replied with her eyes welling up. "I just know he's really sick and Mommy says he needs an operation.

But my Daddy can't pay for it, so I want to use my money."

"How much do you have?" asked the man from Chicago.

"One dollar and eleven cents," Tess answered barely audibly. "And it's all the money I have, but I can get some more if I need to."

"Well, what a coincidence," smiled the man. "A dollar and eleven cents—the exact price of a miracle for little brothers."

He took her money in one hand and with the other hand he grasped her mitten and said, "Take me to where you live. I want to see your brother and meet your parents. Let's see if I have the kind of miracle you need."

That well-dressed man was Dr. Carlton Armstrong, a surgeon, specializing in neurosurgery. The operation was completed without charge and it wasn't long until Andrew was home again and doing well. Mom and Dad were happily talking about the chain of events that had led them to this place.

"That surgery," her Mom whispered, "was a real miracle. I wonder how much it would have cost?"

Tess smiled. She knew exactly how much a miracle cost…one dollar and eleven cents…plus the faith of a little child.

熊孩子

巴兹尔问父亲："爸爸，我能不能出去玩呀？"

"不行，外面正下着雨呢，你出去会感冒的。"他爸爸答道。

"可是，爸爸，我就想出去淋雨。"

父亲放心不下，连忙说："这是我给你买的一本书，你现在乖乖地坐下来好好地看书吧。"

巴兹尔很听话，马上拿起了书，可是刚刚看完第一句，就开始发问了："爸爸，书里面说：一个人跟什么人在一起，就是什么样的人，是真的吗？那，假如一个好人和一个坏人在一起，这个好人会不会因为那个坏人也变成了坏人呢？要不，会不会因为坏人跟好人在一起，就变成好人了呢？要不，就是他们两个人都变了，好人变成了坏人，坏人反倒变成了好人？还有，要是……"

"巴兹尔，"爸爸说道，"你可以出去淋雨啦。"

A Troublesome Child

"Daddy, may I go out?" Asked Basil.

"No, it's raining," answered daddy. "You would catch cold."

"But daddy, I want to go out in the rain."

"Here is a book I've bought you," replied the worried father hastily. "Now sit still and read it."

Basil took the book obediently. But after the first sentence he asked again: "Daddy, it says here: a man is known by the company he keeps. Is that true? Because if a good man keeps company with a bad man, is the good man bad because he keeps company with the bad man, or is the bad man good because he keeps company with the good man, or do they each change, and if the…"

"Basil," said his father, "you may go out in the rain."

圣诞节快乐

两个小男孩在奶奶家过平安夜,临睡前,两个小家伙跪在床边祷告,弟弟扯开嗓子大声喊着自己的愿望。

"我祈祷得到一辆新自行车……

我祈祷得到一部任天堂游戏机……

我祈祷得到一台新的录像机……"

他哥哥靠了过来轻轻推了推他,说道:"你祷告就祷告呗,干吗还大喊大叫的?上帝的耳朵又不背。"弟弟答道:"我也知道上帝的耳朵不背,可奶奶的耳朵背呀!"

Happy Christmas

Two young boys were spending the night before Christmas at their grandma's. At bedtime, the two boys knelt beside their beds to say their prayers when the youngest one began praying at the top of his lungs.

"I pray for a new bicycle...

I pray for a new nintendo...

I pray for a new vcr..."

His older brother leaned over and nudged the younger brother and said, "Why are you shouting your prayers? God isn't deaf." To which the little brother replied, "No, but Gramma is!"

我是你的 BF

一个小男孩对小女孩说:"我是你的 BF。"
天真无邪的小女孩笑嘻嘻地问道:"什么是 BF 呀?"
男孩答道:"是最好的朋友(Best Friend)的意思。"

光阴荏苒,已是经年,他们两情相悦,深情缱绻。
小伙子对姑娘说:"我是你的 BF。"
姑娘羞答答地问道:"什么是 BF 呀?"
小伙子深情款款地凝视着她,说道:"是男朋友(Boy Friend)的意思。"

后来,他们幸运地喜结连理,又喜得贵子。
丈夫笑眯眯地对妻子说:"我是你的 BF。"
妻子柔情似水地问道:"什么是 BF 呀?"
丈夫看了看宝宝,一脸幸福地答道:"是宝宝的父亲(Baby's Father)的意思。"

后来,他们老了。
他们悠闲自在地坐在长椅上。

丈夫笑呵呵地对妻子说道："我的爱，我是你的 BF。"

老太太满是皱纹的脸上露出了微笑，问道："什么是 BF 啊？"

老头答道："是相伴到永远（Be Forever）的意思。"

Do You Know What BF Means

A little boy said to a little girl, "I'm your BF."

The girl asked with an innocent smile on her face, "What is BF?"

"It means Best Friend."

Years later, they fell in love.

The young man said to the young lady, "I am your BF."

She asked him shyly, "What is BF?"

He gazed at her with deep feeling and said, "It means Boy Friend."

Luckily, they got married and had a baby.

The husband said to his wife smilingly, "I am your BF."

The wife asked tenderly, "What is BF?"

The husband looked at the baby and said happily, "Baby's Father."

Then, they were old.

They were sitting on the bench leisurely.

The old man said, "My love, I am your BF."

The old lady asked with a smile on her wrinkled face, "What is BF?"

"Be Forever!"

天作之合

我在公共汽车站碰到了加布。我当时的情绪有些低落。在刚刚过去的那个漫长的一周里,各方各面各种倒霉各种不顺。

"你看起来心事重重的嘛,宝贝。"他漫不经心地说道。

"太无礼啦。"我心中暗想,抬起头来看到了他那双我所见过的最阳光的蓝眼睛。我的目光并没有停留在他的蓝眼睛上,他的身材也可以与我在大学里所研究过的任何一个希腊神像媲美。

正常情况下,我不是热衷于爱情小说里描述的那种人,可是,他阳光般金黄色的卷发更衬托出我面前这玉树临风的完美身材。他下身穿着随意的蓝色牛仔裤,上身穿的白色丝绸衬衫在微风中泛起涟漪。

我打了个激灵,从那个瞬间的遐想回到了现实中来,意识到自己刚才一定在傻乎乎地盯着他看来着。"哦,上帝,对不起……"我开了口。

"对不起,詹妮,让你失望了,我不是上帝,"他笑道,"我是加布,不是上帝。"

我们的四目交汇,迸发出一串咯咯的笑声。那一刻,我知道有特别的事情发生了。

我本来是想做个自我介绍来着,随即意识到他已经叫过我的名字,一个可怕的念头在我脑海里闪现。

"你是怎么知道我名字的?该不是萨拉又调皮捣蛋搞那个什么

天作之合游戏吧？失败了几次以后，我还以为她已经淡了，已经放弃了呢！"

加布若有所思，做了个鬼脸，很滑稽。"我可不认识什么萨拉。"他说着，拿出了一个翻得很烂的黑色通讯录。我注意到了通讯录封皮上的银色机翼徽章，原来他是个飞行员呢！我可真幸运！

他仔细地查看目录S，"没有，我的朋友里没有叫萨拉的。"他咧开嘴笑了。

我也咧开嘴笑了，我顺着他的目光看到了我罩衫上别的铜制胸配上的名字，那是我所工作的大型百货商店化妆品专柜配发的工装的一部分。

"我猜你不叫埃斯蒂就叫詹妮。"他的微笑这么迷人。

就在这时，我等的公共汽车不合时宜地来了。我把谨慎小心都丢进了风里，在一个香水小样纸片上用口红匆匆写下了我的电话号码。"给我打电话，加布，也就是假如……当然……假如你不……"

可是，时间已经不够了。我跳上已经启动了的公共汽车，透过车窗看着他，可是他已经走了。

我为什么要上这趟车？我可真是个大傻瓜！肯定还有另一趟车呀，可是还会有另一个加布吗？

还有，我不敢肯定他会不会给我打电话。那天上午剩下的时间在慢慢地过去，我也一直在用我当时应该怎么做来折磨自己，想着如果我这样或者那样做会有什么结果……

"詹妮！请不要胡思乱想了，有顾客来了，快去接待。"我的领班的声音突然把我的思绪带回了现实。

我的心跳了起来。

"不好意思，今天早晨一位漂亮的女士给了我一个'天使雾'香水的样品……"

是他，是加布。

"你什么时候下班，詹妮，"他问道。"你能跟我在华伦天奴见面吗？你知道那里吗？"

我不知所措，结结巴巴，尴尬得不知说什么好，我的主管再次出现在我身边也无济于事。

"詹妮，我们到这里不是社交来的。"她严厉地教训道。

可是加布的魅力在她身上也起效了。"亲爱的女士，"他说道，"亲爱的女士，我想要你们最大瓶的'天使雾'香水。"

她大喜过望，急忙去存量室去取。

还是那种咧嘴一笑，这个男人说什么能让人拒绝？

"加布，你不必买那个的……"那香水贵得惊人。

"可是我要买，詹妮。请用礼盒包好，今晚带到华伦天奴去。我跟那里的老板有约，所以现在得马上走。"

他付了香水钱，给了我一个飞吻就走了。

时间过得真慢，五点钟终于到了。整整一下午，我的心都在翻江倒海，紧张得胡思乱想。最后，到了华伦天奴门口的时候，我却犹豫了，我担心他没来。推开转门，我在拥挤的一张张桌子间寻找他的白肤金发。

他在那里。

可是他跟一个男人谈兴正浓！我的心不由得一沉，我还实心眼儿地以为只有我们两个人呢。

他抬起头来，我迅速用微笑来掩饰自己失望的心情。他大踏步走了过来，把我领到了那张桌子旁边，给我拉开椅子请我坐下，内外兼修，完美的绅士，我想。

"詹妮，这是内森。内森，詹妮。"他轻松自在地把我介绍给他的朋友。

内森很愧疚。"对不起，打扰你们了。"这是他说的第一句话。

"没什么，没什么，我一点儿也不在意。"我尽量优雅地假意说道。

侍者过来等我们点菜，在讲解特色菜的同时把亚麻餐巾上的马铃薯屑抖掉。

内森可能是意识到了自己的存在造成了潜在的尴尬，于是站起身来。"谢谢你的建议，加布，换一个角度看待这个问题很有意义。认识你很高兴，詹妮，过一个美好的夜晚吧。"

连他的朋友都如此完美！

"你不必走啊，内森，詹妮不会在意的，毕竟我们还有一生的时间来互相了解。"

又是那样咧嘴一笑，我怎么能拒绝这样一个男人的任何要求？况且他最后说明听起来就像是承诺！

"对的，内森，请你留下来。"我尽量说得真诚。

内森在迟疑，而加布却很坚持，所以内森最后让了步又在椅子上坐了下来。"嗯，我也是饿坏了。"

"我推荐大鱼盘配你吃过的最美味的硬面包，一瓶山脊蒙特－贝罗园霞多丽干白葡萄酒佐餐。"加布漂亮的蓝眼睛闪着幸福的光。

那顿饭好吃极了。事实证明，内森也是一个好饭友。我还以为内森一定是加布的同事，可是很快就明白了，他们就是在饭店认识的，就是在加布等我的时候认识的。

内森上个星期很难过——跟我一模一样！——所以很愿意跟这个友善的陌生人说话。说到把我们带到一起共进晚餐的机缘巧合，我们都哈哈大笑。

吃饭的时候，我和内森都发现我们对希腊神话有共同的兴趣。我吃惊地发现我们上大学时候还是同班同学呢，太巧啦！

我们一起说说笑笑，几个小时过去了，我发现自己与内森的共同点越来越多，对加布的迷恋却越来越淡，我发现内森的思想深沉而敏锐，与加布的外在美一样迷人。

晚上晚些时候，我们的谈话被那个小心翼翼地在加布旁边徘徊的侍者打断了。

"对不起，加布里埃尔先生，有个电话找您。"

加布不在的时候，我和内森聊得轻松自在，我觉得跟内森在一起更放松，不像跟加布在一起想想都紧张。

几分钟以后，加布回来了，我几乎都觉得有些失望了。他咧嘴一笑，以一种或者另一种形式，带着歉意。

"是老板打来的，有一件要事，我恐怕就要把你们撂在这里了。账单我已经付了。"他转身就走。

"加布，等等！你的'天使雾'香水，"我一边叫他，一边在我的包里翻找那个包装盒。

"哦，对，那当然是给你的，詹妮，如果你愿意接受的话。"

这让我始料未及。"我不能接受，不能，这太贵重啦。"

"可以的，你可以接受的，"他坚定地说道。接着，他说了句蹊跷的话。"婚礼上用，詹妮。"

然后，他就走了。

我和内森慢慢地喝着咖啡。他非常腼腆地问我，愿不愿意在这个周末出游，参观一些历史悠久的教堂。

"我不愿意让你以为我是个自命不凡的人什么的，詹妮，可我对建筑是真爱，我特别想去看看圣保罗大教堂新装的彩色玻璃窗，显而易见，这里面有故事。"

我的胃口被吊了起来。"什么故事？"

"是这样，当地教区的居民自费安装的，其中有几个人认为在自己的烦恼人生中得到过天使的帮助——你知道，那些运气不太好的人，觉得情绪低落，他们把这些彩色玻璃作为一种供奉献给帮助过他们的天使。"

"多么感人的故事，内森！我会去的，一定会很有趣。"

星期六早晨，内森到了我家门前，备了一个野餐篮子和一瓶香槟。"庆祝一下我们的相识。"他说道。

在车里，他问我可有加布的消息。我说没有，还加了一句。"我接受了那瓶香水，觉得自己像个骗子，香水那么贵，可我没有他的电话，道声谢都不能。"

圣保罗大教堂很美。我们在长长的汽车道上行驶，我不禁大声感叹道，"这就是我梦寐以求的结婚的教堂！"

话音未落，我随即绯红了脸，而内森似乎却没有感到不安。

穿过带有雕刻的一道道门，我们为古建筑的优雅而惊叹不已。教堂得到了忠实的还原，装饰得异常华丽。

高大石柱的顶上有小天使守护着安宁和平，可是真正让我屏息静气的却是彩色玻璃窗。

我和内森一起站在壮丽辉煌的彩色玻璃下面，仰望着这熟悉的面孔。牛仔裤和真丝衬衫已经替换成了飞扬的白袍和巨大的翅膀。

可是，毫无疑问，这就是加布。加布里埃尔先生手里拿着一个黑色小通讯录，封皮上就有银色的翅膀。

Made in Heaven

I met Gabe one day at the bus stop. I was feeling kind of low. It had been a long week of disappointments and misadventures in all directions.

"You look as if you have the weight of the world on your shoulders, babe," he said casually.

"How rude," I thought, until I looked up into the most glorious blue eyes I had ever seen. It didn't stop there. His physique rivalled that of any of the Greek gods whose antics I had studied at college.

Normally, I'm not the type to go in for romance novel descriptions, but the sun-streaked, wavy blond hair set off the perfect body standing before my eyes. He was dressed in casual blue jeans and a white silk shirt that rippled in the breeze.

Coming back to earth with a start, I realized I must have been gawping at him. I felt an idiot. "Oh, God, I'm sorry…" I began.

"Sorry to disappoint you, Jenny," he smiled, "but I'm Gabe, not God."

Our eyes met and we both exploded into giggles. At that moment, I knew something special had happened.

I thought to introduce myself, and then realized that he had already called me by name. An awful thought crossed my mind.

"How did you know my name? It's not Sarah doing her match-made-in-heaven trick again? That's beginning to wear a bit thin after seven failed attempts. I thought she would have given up!"

Gabe pulled a comically thoughtful face. "I don't think I know Sarah," he said, pulling out a very tattered black book. I noticed the silver wings emblem on the cover. He was an airline pilot! Lucky me!

He made a rather elaborate show of checking the "S" index. "Nope, not one of mine," he grinned.

I grinned, too, when I followed his eyes to the bronze name tag pinned to my blouse. It was part of the uniform at the perfumery counter of the large department store where I worked.

"Jenny was my first guess after Estee." He had such an engaging smile!

At that moment, my bus made an illtimed arrival. Throwing caution to the wind, I scribbled my phone number on the back of a perfume sample card with a lipstick. "Call me, Gabe, that's if…of course…if you don't…"

But there was no more time. Jumping on the departing bus, I

looked for him through the window, but he was gone.

Why did I get on that bus? What an idiot I was! There would always be another bus. But another Gabe?

And, of course, I was not at all sure that he would call me. The rest of the morning dragged on as I tormented myself with what I should have done. Wondering what could have happened if…

"Jenny! Get your head down out of the clouds, please. There's a customer to serve." It was my supervisor bringing me back to reality with jolt.

And my heart leapt.

"Excuse me, I was given a sample of 'Angel Mist' by a beautiful young lady this morning…"

It was him. It was Gabe.

"What time do you finish, Jenny," he asked. "Will you meet me at Valentino's? Do you know it?"

I was overwhelmed and stumbled embarrassingly over my words. It didn't help when the supervisor suddenly appeared again beside me.

"Jenny. We are not here to socialize," she admonished sternly.

But Gabe's charm worked on her, too. "Dear lady," he said, "dear lady, I would like to purchase your largest bottle of 'Angel Mist'."

And she scuttled off delightedly to the stock room.

There was that grin again. How could I refuse this man anything?

"Gabe, you don't have to buy it..." It was a shockingly expensive purchase.

"But I do, Jenny. Please gift-wrap it and bring it to Valentino's tonight. I have an appointment with the boss so I have to dash."

He paid for the perfume, blew me a kiss and was gone.

Five o'clock couldn't come quickly enough. All afternoon my stomach danced with nervous anticipation. At last, outside Valentino's, I hesitated, worried that he might not be there. Pushing through the revolving doors, I searched the crowded tables for the white-blond mane of hair.

He was there.

But he was deep in conversation with another man! My heart sank. I had honestly thought that we would be alone!

He looked up and I quickly hid my disappointment with a smile. He strode over and ushered me to the table. The perfect gentleman to match the looks, I thought, as he held the chair for me while I sat down.

"Jenny, this is Nathan. Nathan, Jenny." He introduced me to his friend with easy charm.

Nathan was apologetic. "I'm sorry to intrude here," were his first words.

"No, no, I don't mind at all." I lied as graciously as I could.

The waiter came to take our order, shaking out the crisp linen napkins as he explained the specials.

Nathan began to stand up, perhaps realizing the potential awkwardness of his presence. "Thanks for the advice, Gabe. It makes sense looking at it from that angle. Nice to have met you, Jenny, have a lovely evening."

Even his friends were perfect!

"You don't have to leave, Nathan. Jenny won't mind. After all, we've got a whole lifetime ahead of us to get to know each other."

There was that grin again. How could I refuse this man anything? And his last comment sounded promising!

"Yes, Nathan. Please stay." I managed to sound quite genuine.

Nathan was uncertain, but Gabe was insistent. He gave in and settled back in his chair. "Well, I am rather famished."

"I can recommend the fish platter served with the most delicious damper you have ever tasted. A bottle of Monte Vicarto Chardonnay to accompany." Gabe's beautiful blue eyes were bright with happiness.

The meal was superb. And Nathan proved to be good company. I had thought that Nathan must be one of Gabe's work colleagues, but it soon emerged that they had only met in the restaurant while Gabe was waiting for me.

Nathan had been having a difficult week—just like me!—and welcomed his conversation with the friendly stranger. We all had a good laugh over the chance encounters that had brought us all to have dinner together.

Over dinner, Nathan and I uncovered our mutual interest in Greek mythology. I was amazed to find that he had been in the same class as myself at college. What a coincidence!

We talked and laughed together for hours and my infatuation with Gabe faded as I noticed how much Nathan and I had in common. There was a depth and sensitivity to him that I found as attractive as Gabe's physical beauty.

Later on during the evening, our conversation was interrupted by the waiter hovering discreetly at Gabe's side.

"Excuse me, Mr. Gabriel, there is a telephone call for you."

Nathan and I chatted easily during Gabe's absence. I felt very relaxed with him, quite unlike the nervous anticipation I felt with Gabe.

I was almost disappointed when Gabe returned after a few minutes. His grin, which seemed to be permanent in one form or another, was apologetic.

"That was the boss. Something important has come up, so I'm afraid I'll have to leave you to it. I've paid the bill." He turned to go.

"Gabe, wait! Your 'Angel Mist'," I called to him, rummaging in my bag for the package.

"Oh, yes, it's for you of course, Jenny, if you'll accept it."

I hadn't even suspected. "I couldn't. No, it's too much."

"Yes, you could," he said firmly. And then he said something very strange. "Wear it at your wedding, Jenny."

Then he was gone.

Nathan and I lingered over coffee. He asked, rather shyly, if I would like to come on a tour of historic churches at the weekend.

"I don't want you to think I'm a stuffed shirt or anything, Jen, but I really love architecture. St Pat's has a new stained glass window which I'm dying to see. Apparently there is quite a story attached to it."

I was intrigued. "What's the story?"

"Well, the local parishioners paid for it themselves. A few of them believed they had received angelic help in their troubled lives—you know, people a bit down on their luck, feeling a bit low. They had the window made as a sort of tribute to the angel who helped them."

"What a great story, Nathan! I'll come. It might be fun."

On Saturday morning, Nathan arrived at my door armed with a picnic basket and a bottle of champagne. "To celebrate our meeting," he said.

In the car, he asked if I had heard from Gabe. I had to say no, adding. "I feel a fraud, accepting that perfume. It was so expensive. But I don't have his number so I can't even thank him."

The church was beautiful. As we drove up the long driveway, I couldn't help exclaiming, "This is just the sort of church I dreamed of getting married in!"

I blushed immediately, but Nathan didn't seem perturbed.

Entering through the great carved doors, we marvelled at the ancient grace of the building. It had been faithfully restored and was very ornate.

Stone cherubim kept a peaceful watch from atop the mighty columns, but it was the stained glass window that truly took my breath away.

Nathan and I stood together beneath the glorious colored glass and looked up at the familiar features. The silk shirt and jeans had been replaced by flowing white robes and huge sweeping wings.

But, unmistakably, it was Gabe. Mr. Gabriel, holding his little black book with the silver wings on the cover.

冬 夜

一个寒冷的冬夜。在空寂无人的马路旁边，疏枝交横的树下，候着末班车的，只有我孤零零的一个人。虽然不远的墙根下，也蹲有一团黑影，但事实证明他只是一个流浪乞丐。街道两旁，是一排排灯火辉煌的别墅，对着深蓝的天空无声地微笑着。一阵阵凄厉的风吹过，街道上冷冰冰的。紧紧地抱着树枝不放的一两片枯叶，也不时发出凄惨的沙沙声。

那团蹲着的黑影，接了我的一枚铜板，嘴里说着谢谢，一面高兴地站起来跟我搭讪，一面抱怨着天气："真冷呀，再没有比这里更冷了！……先生，你说是不是？"

看见他并不是个讨厌的老头儿，我就也乐意回应他："乡下怕更要冷些吧？"

"不，不，"他不同意我的意见，却咳嗽起来，要说出的话，堵在喉咙里了。

我说："为什么？只要下了霜，你就会发现，乡下的房屋和田野清早就蒙上一层白霜，这城里的街上却一点也看不见。"

他捶了几下胸口，来缓解缓解咳嗽，兴奋地接着说道："那是，那是……乡下冷，你往人家门前的稻草堆上一钻就暖了呀……这街上，哼，鬼地方！……大山里呵，比乡下更冷哩，可是烧上堆火，全家人团团围坐，那就是天堂啊！"

接着他便说起壮年之日,冬夜在南方那些山里流浪的故事。我对漂泊生活是很感兴趣的,既然我等的车又没来,于是就怂恿他说下去,他说:"晚上在那些山里,只要你是一个正经人,你就可以朝有灯火闪烁的人家走去,迎着犬吠声,敲开树荫下的柴门,长驱直入,不必犹豫。用手分开火堆周围的人们,管他是男是女,把你带着风霜的又湿又冷的身子置身于他们中间。而烤红薯和热茶的香味,就一下子扑鼻而来了。"

"环顾四周,一张张友善的面孔对你微笑着,丝毫没有怪你唐突的神情。你刚开口说由哪儿来的时候,一杯热热的浓茶,就递到了你面前。老奶奶吩咐她的孙女,快加些柴火,说是客人需要火更旺些,才能把身子暖过来;等你身子暖和过来了,也消了乏以后,你可以轻轻捏捏小孩子的脸蛋儿,做个鬼脸,逗他们咯咯地笑。年轻的妈妈一高兴,就会怂恿她的孩子把正要吃的红薯跟你分享,小孩子就会一分两半,塞到你这位客人的手里。如果你要在他们家过夜,他们会尽心竭力殷勤地招待你。倘若你只是想歇歇脚,暖暖身子,还要赶路的话,他们还会送你到大门口,嘴里念叨着,'回来的时候一定要再来呀!'"老头子还在喋喋不休,一阵冷风吹来,就又咳嗽起来,我正听得津津有味,都忘记了冷,突然,老头子忘记了我们本是陌生人,一把抓住了我的手,问道:

"先生,你能告诉我为什么吗?……这里的人家,火一定更大更旺,看窗子多么亮哪……他们为什么不准一个外地人进去烤烤手呢?"

公共汽车从远处轰隆隆地开过来了,我赶忙抽出了手,扯开嗓门儿喊道:"因为他们比山里人更文明……"

待我跳进灯火通明的公共汽车里,车随即启动了,蓦地离开那个老头子。然而,在遥远的南国群山里,油灯闪烁的小小人家里面,那些丰美的醉人的温暖和那些居民的友善,却深深地留存在了我的记忆里。

A Winter Night

It was a cold winter night. The street was deserted. I stood alone under a tree with an entanglement of bare branches overhead, waiting for the last bus to arrive. A few paces off in the darkness there was a shadowy figure squatting against the wall, but he turned out to be a tramp. The street was lined with fine houses, their illuminated windows beaming quietly towards the dark blue sky. It was icy cold with a gust of strong wind howling around. A couple of withered leaves, still clinging to the branches, rustled mournfully from time to time.

The shadowy figure, taking a copper coin from me with thanks, straightened up to attempt a conversation with me. "It's really cold here," he complained. "It couldn't be colder anywhere else…What do you think, sir?"

Seeing that he was not too nasty an old man, I readily responded: "It must be colder in the country, I'm afraid."

"No, no," he disagreed and began to cough, his words stuck up in his throat.

"Why?" I asked. "In the country when it frosts, you always

find the roofs and the fields turning white in the morning, but you don't see that here on the streets."

He patted his chest to ease off his coughing and went on excitedly: "True, true...it's cold in the country, but when you get into somebody's straw stack, you are warm again at once... But this street, humm, what a terrible place! In the mountains, it's even colder, but when they have a fire in the house with the whole family sitting around it, wow, it's heaven!"

Then he began to relate to me the adventures of his younger days-travelling alone in winter nights through the mountains in the south. As I was interested in stories about wanderers and since the bus had not arrived yet, I encouraged him to go on. "When you end up in the mountains at night," he said, "and if you are a decent person, you can always turn to the place where there is a light flickering and a dog barking. You push open the bramble gate under the shade and walk in without hesitation. Part the people, men or women, around the fire with your hands and you bring yourself—a cold and wet man with dew-among them. Immediately your nose is filled with the aroma of hot tea and roast sweet potatoes."

"When you look round you see friendly faces smiling at you, there is no hint of anything like blame for what elsewhere might be considered as brusqueness. Scarcely have you begun to tell them where you come from when a cup of hot and strong tea is handed over to you. Grandma will tell her granddaughter to feed the fire with more wood, saying that the guest needs more beat to warm up. When you are recovered from cold and fatigue, you tend to tease the baby, stroking his chin, giving a gentle pinch to his cheek or making a face to provoke him to gurgle. The delighted young mother will encourage her baby to share his sweet potato with you. The baby will then break it in two and thrust one half into your hand. If you intend to stay overnight, you will be entertained with all possible hospitality. If you've just dropped in to warm up and then go on your way, they will see you off at the gate, saying 'Please do drop in on us again on your way back.'" In the middle of his babbling another gust of wind brushed by and the old man began to cough again. I was so intrigued by his story that I did not feel the cold any more. Suddenly he grabbed my hand, forgetting that we were strangers, and asked:

"Sir, could you tell me why the people here even do not allow a countryman in to warm his hands? They must've got bigger fires in their houses. Look at their bright windows..."

The bus came rumbling up. Withdrawing my hand from his, I answered at the top of my voice, "Because they are more civilized than the mountain people..."

With that I jumped onto the brightly-lit bus which started moving on, leaving the old man behind. But the little houses with flickering oil lamps in the remote mountains and the intoxicating warmth and friendliness of their inhabitants left a deep impress on my memory.

爱上老师

保罗·维拉德

本森小姐是世界上最亲切、最可爱、最美丽的人。她是我二年级的老师,我长大了一定要娶她——只要她肯等我。我常常整整一个上午在座位上扭来扭去憋着,就是不举手,不去上厕所。有她在教室,每一分每一秒都宝贵,我不能错过。

但是,老师如果问谁愿意擦黑板,谁愿意收卷子交到讲台上,我总是头一个举手。这可是最美的差事了。可以撇开班上的同学,接近她,我会把卷子理了又理,叠放得整整齐齐,才依依不舍地回到座位上去。

开学不久,我就缠着我妈要她在我的午饭盒里多放一个苹果或桃子。我一直没敢说这是给老师的,也一直没敢把我的这些礼物当面送给本森小姐。每天都有好吃的东西偷偷地放在讲台上。她每天的反应也是一样。

本森小姐会走进教室,坐下来,说道:"小朋友们早!"

"本森小姐早!"全班齐声回答。

"哈,真好!"她拿起当天的礼物,然后东张西望,"是哪个贴心的小朋友给我送的呀?"

谁也没争这份功,我就更不可能。我低着头,两眼盯着书桌。

她会问:"是不是有人暗恋我啊?"

我都感觉得到脸红了起来。我肯定大家都在盯着我,只见老师把水果放在一边,开始讲课,我这才松了口气。

一个秋天的上午,全班兴奋地沸腾起来。原来有人发现,第二天,也就是星期五,是本森小姐的生日。人人都想送件礼物给她。我的心都快蹦出来了:终于可以名正言顺地送她东西了。那天下午,我一直在田野里搜寻野花。那个季节已经没有多少开着的野花了,不过我还是在灌木丛里找到了好几种鲜艳的浆果,找到了一些干枯的蓟花头。后来我还看到在一小块地里,有一片色彩艳丽的红叶……

第二天早晨,大家都纷纷呈上自己的礼物,我拖到最后才走上讲台,把一束花送给了老师。

她接过花,开心地叫了起来,还在脸上贴了一会儿。她对我报以一笑,还拍了拍我的头。

接下去那个星期一,本森小姐没来上课。上午过了一半了,我被叫到校长室去。我一进去,惊讶地看到了我妈。桌上还放着我送给本森小姐的那束花。

"你知道本森小姐今天去哪儿了?"校长问我。

"不知道,先生。"我答道。

"本森小姐在医院,是你把她送进去的!"校长一字一顿地清晰地说道。

我一屁股坐在椅子上,吓坏了。

"你知道你给她送的是什么东西吗?"他又问道。

我点点头。"有浆果、蓟花,还有挺好看的红叶。"我一一列举道。

"小家伙,那些'挺好看的红叶'就是毒葛,年轻人。"(毒葛是一种苏模叶,直接接触可引发严重的皮疹。)他越说越生气,"你摘的时候采取什么保护措施了？你戴手套了吗？"

我摇了摇头。"真的，我不知道是毒葛。"我哭了起来。

校长站起身。"保罗，我罚你停学十天。十天后复学，以观后效。"

我一路抽抽搭搭地回了家。倒不是因为停学，是因为意中人惨遭不幸。我跑到树林里摘了些野葛叶子，拿回家给妈看。"您看，"我忍着眼泪说，"我手上根本没有戴什么呀！"

妈看看野葛叶子。"赶快丢到垃圾桶里去，宝贝。然后把手好好洗干净。"

我洗手回来，我妈正坐在摇椅上。她伸开双臂，把我搂在怀里坐在她腿上摇了几分钟。

"我们好好玩一次吧！"她最后大声说道，"你最想做什么？"

"我想去看本森小姐。"我回答道。

我们到了医院，只见本森小姐坐在病床上，脸上缠满了绷带，只露出一只眼睛，两只手也裹着绷带。

"我不知道那是毒葛，"我的话脱口而出，"我不是有意伤害您。我就想送您一点东西……"我说不下去了，强忍着泪水。

本森小姐那只眼仔细地看着我。"你想送我一点特别的东西，对吧，保罗？"我点点头。

"那些苹果也都是你送的，是不是？"我又点点头。

"等我拆掉绷带，"她说，"我要好好地拥抱你。"

我感觉到无上的幸福。她没生我的气啊。

"保罗，我还要告诉你一个天大的秘密，"她又说了下去，"等我结了婚，要是有个儿子，我就要他长大了和你一个样。"

妈妈领我走出病房的时候，我仿佛看到本森小姐的那只眼里闪烁着泪花。

A Bouquet for Miss Benson

By Paul Villiard

Miss Benson was the kindest, sweetest, most beautiful person that ever walked the earth. She was my second-grade teacher, and I was going to marry her when I grew up—if she would wait. I would sit squirming in my seat for the entire morning to keep from raising my hand. I could not bear to miss one precious moment of her presence by leaving the room.

My hand was always the first to be raised, however, when Miss Benson called for volunteers to clean the blackboards or to gather papers and bring them to her desk. That was the best chore of all. It made possible getting near enough to her to close out the others in the classroom. I would arrange and rearrange the papers. They had to be in perfect order before I would make my reluctant way back to my seat.

Early in the term, I started asking my mother to put an extra apple or peach in my lunch. I never quit worked up the courage to say it was for my teacher, as I never quite worked up the courage to hand my gift to her directly. Each day the delicacy found its way unobserved to the corner of her desk. And each day the response was the same.

Miss Benson would come in and sit down. "Good morning, children."

"Good morning, Miss Benson." in unison.

"Why, how nice!" She would pick up the offering of the day, then look around the room. "What thoughtful little boy or girl brought me this?"

No one claimed the honor, least of all me. I kept my head down, looking at my desk.

"Can it be that I have a secret admirer?" she would ask.

I would feel the red rising in my face. I was certain that everyone was looking at me, and I would sigh with relief when Miss Benson put the fruit away and started the lesson.

One fall morning, the class was abuzz with excitement. Someone had discovered that the next day, Friday, was Miss Benson's birthday. Everyone wanted to get her a present. My heart gave a leap, at last I could give her something, openly. That afternoon was spent combing the fields for wild flowers. Not many were in bloom at that time of year, but I found several kinds of height berries on shrubs, some dry thistle heads. And finally I came upon a patch of gorgeous crimson leaves…

In the morning I hung back as others presented their gifts.

Finally I went to the desk and gave the bouquet to Miss Benson.

She exclaimed with pleasure as she look it, and held it to her cheek for a moment. My reward was a smile and a pat on the head.

The next Monday, Miss Benson was not in class. About the middle of the morning, I was asked to go to the principal's office. When I arrived, I was surprised to see my mother. On a table was my bouquet.

"Do you know where Miss Benson is today?" the principal asked.

"No, sir," I answered.

"Miss Benson." he said, slowly and clearly, "is in the hospital, and you sent her there!"

I sat, stricken, in my chair.

"Do you know what you gave her?" he continued.

I nodded. "Berries, thistles and pretty red leaves." I listed.

"Those 'pretty red leaves' are poison ivy, young man." (Poison ivy is a kind of sumac which can cause a severe skin rash if touched) His voice was filling with anger. "How did you protect yourself when you picked them? Gloves?"

I shook my head. "Honest, I didn't know they were poison ivy." I started to cry.

The principal stood up. "Paul, I am suspending you for ten days. What happens after that depends upon your behavior when you return."

I sniffed all the way home. Not because I had been put out of school, but because of the appalling tragedy to my lady love. I went to the woods to pick posion-ivy leaves and show them to my mother. "You see," I said, holding back the tears, "I didn't wear anything at all."

Mother looked at the leaves. "Put them in the garbage can, honey. Then wash your hands real well."

When I went back, Mother was sitting in her rocker, she held out her arms, and I sat in her lap while she rocked me for a few minutes.

"Let's have a party!" she exclaimed finally. "What would you like to do the very most?"

"I'd like to go to see Miss Benson." I replied.

Miss Benson was sitting up in bed when we arrived. Her face was covered with bandages. Only one eye was showing. Both of her hands were swathed as well.

"I didn't know they were poison ivy," I blurted out. "I didn't mean to make you sick. I only wanted to give you something…" I stopped talking and swallowed hard.

Miss Benson's one eye studied me. "You wanted to give me something special, didn't you Paul?" I nodded.

"All those apples were from you, weren't they?" Again I nodded.

"When I get these bandages off," she said, "I am going to

give you a great big hug."

I was filled with happiness. She was not mad at me.

"And I'll tell you a great big secret, too. Paul," she continued, "When I am married, if I have a son, I would like him to grow up just like you."

I wasn't certain that I saw a tear in her eye as Mother led me out of the room.

所谓成长，无非是所见即所得

多萝西·劳·诺特

在批评中长大的孩子，会学会吹毛求疵。
在敌意中长大的孩子，会学会明争暗斗。
在恐惧中长大的孩子，会学会杞人忧天。
在怜悯中长大的孩子，会感觉顾影自怜。
在嘲笑中长大的孩子，会感觉缩手缩脚。
在猜忌中长大的孩子，会感觉嫉贤妒能。
在羞辱中长大的孩子，会感觉自惭形秽。
在鼓励中长大的孩子，会学会信心十足。
在宽容中长大的孩子，会学会襟怀宽广。
在赞扬中长大的孩子，会学会品鉴欣赏。
在接纳中长大的孩子，会学会仁者爱人。
在认可中长大的孩子，会学会不坠青云之志。
在分享中长大的孩子，会学会慷慨大方。
在诚信中长大的孩子，会学会待人真诚。
在公平中长大的孩子，会学会刚正不阿。

在仁慈和体贴中长大的孩子，会学会尊重他人。

在安全中长大的孩子，会学会对周围的人对自己，都深信不疑。

在友善中长大的孩子，会感觉这个世界简直是美好的人间天堂。

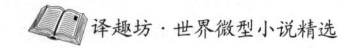

Children Learn What They Live

By Dorothy Law Nolte

If children live with criticism, they learn to condemn.

If children live with hostility, they learn to fight.

If children live with fear, they learn to be apprehensive.

If children live with pity, they learn to feel sorry for themselves.

If children live with ridicule, they learn to feel shy.

If children live with jealousy, they learn to feel envy.

If children live with shame, they learn to feel guilty.

If children live with encouragement, they learn confidence.

If children live with tolerance, they learn patience.

If children live with praise, they learn appreciation.

If children live with acceptance, they learn to love.

If children live with approval, they learn to like themselves.

If children live with recognition, they learn it is good to have a goal.

If children live with sharing, they learn generosity.

If children live with honesty, they learn truthfulness.

If children live with fairness, they learn justice.

If children live with kindness and consideration, they learn respect.

If children live with security, they learn to have faith in themselves and in those about them.

If children live with friendliness, they learn the world is a nice place in which to live.

生　活

生活是机遇，受益无穷吧。

生活是美妙，眼慕手追吧。

生活是挑战，迎难而上吧。

生活是职责，尽职尽责吧。

生活是游戏，尽兴玩耍吧。

生活是承诺，说到做到吧。

生活是悲伤，转悲为喜吧。

生活是首歌，放声欢唱吧。

生活是挣扎，听之任之吧。

生活是悲剧，直面正视吧。

生活是探险，放胆去闯吧。

生活是命运，掌控在手吧。

生活诚珍贵，幸勿自毁之。

生活其实就是生活，为生活而战吧！

Life

Life is an opportunity, benefit from it.

Life is beauty, admire it.

Life is a challenge, meet it.

Life is a duty, complete it.

Life is a game, play it.

Life is a promise, fulfill it.

Life is sorrow, overcome it.

Life is a song, sing it.

Life is a struggle, accept it.

Life is a tragedy, confront it.

Life is an adventure, dare it.

Life is luck, make it.

Life is too precious, do not destroy it.

Life is life, fight for it.

玫瑰之约

道格·贝尔

约翰·布兰查德从长凳上站起身来,整了整军装,仔细地观察着格兰德中央车站进出的人群。

他在寻找一位姑娘,一位佩戴玫瑰的姑娘。他了解她的内心,但不了解她的长相。十二个月前,在佛罗里达州的一个图书馆,他对她产生了兴趣。他从书架上取下了一本书,很快便被吸引住了,不是被书的内容吸引,而是被铅笔写的眉批吸引了,那柔和的笔迹显示出一颗善于思考的心灵和具有洞见的头脑。

在书的卷首,他发现了书前主人的姓名——霍利斯·梅奈尔小姐。他耗时费力地找到了她的地址。她住在纽约市。他给她写了一封信自我介绍了一下,还请她回信。第二天他被轮船运到了海外,在第二次世界大战中服役。

在接下来的一年里,两个人通过鸿雁传书来往增进了了解。每一封信都像一颗种子撒入肥沃的心灵之土。浪漫的爱情之花含苞待放。布兰查德提出要一张照片,可她拒绝了。她解释道:"如果你对我的感情基础是真情实感的,是诚心诚意的,那我的长相好坏并不重要。设想我形容美丽。我将会一直深感不安,唯恐你只是以貌取人,盲目相爱,而这种爱情令我憎恶。设想我相貌平平,其貌不扬(你得承认,更有可能性是这样)。那我一直会担心,你和我保持通信仅仅是出于孤独寂寞,无人交谈。不,不要要照片。等你到了纽约,你会见到我,到时你可再作决定。切记,见面后我俩都可以自由决定中止关系或继续交往——无论你怎么选择……"

他从欧洲回国的日子终于到了。他们安排了两个人的第一次约会——晚上7点,在纽约格兰德中央车站。

"你会认出我的,"她写道,"我会在衣襟上戴一朵红玫瑰。"于是,晚上7点,他在车站,寻找一位过去的十二个月里在自己生活中占据了如此特殊地位的姑娘,一位素未谋面,但其文字伴随着他、始终支撑着他的姑娘。

下面,就让布兰查德先生本人告诉你接下来发生的事吧:

一位年轻的姑娘向我走来,她身材修长苗条。一头卷曲的金发披在秀美的耳后。她的眼睛碧蓝如花。她的双唇和下颌线条既柔和又坚定。她身穿浅绿色套装,宛若春天的化身。

我朝她走去,彻底忘了去看她有没有戴玫瑰花。

我走过去时,她双唇绽开挑逗的微笑。"和我同路吗,水兵?"她小声问道。我情不自禁,再向她走近一步。可就在这时,我看到了霍利斯·梅奈尔。她差不多就站在姑娘的正后面,早已年过四十,灰白的头发塞进一顶旧帽子里。

她体态臃肿,多肉的双脚挤进一双低跟鞋里。

穿着绿色套装的姑娘快步走开了。我觉得自己好像被撕裂成了两半,一方面热切地想去追赶那个姑娘,另一方面我又渴望那一位以其心灵真诚陪伴我并成为我的精神支柱的女人。

而她站在那儿,苍白的圆脸显得温柔理智,灰色的眼睛闪耀着温暖亲切的光辉。我没有迟疑。

我手里紧握着那本小小的让她辨认我的蓝色羊皮面旧书。这不会是爱情,但将是某种珍贵的或许比爱情更美妙的东西,一种我曾经感激,并将永远感激的友情。

我挺胸站立,敬了个礼,并举起手中的书好让那位女士看。不过在我开口说话的时候,失望的痛苦几乎使我窒息。"我是约翰·布兰查德中尉,想必您就是梅奈尔小姐。很高兴您来见我。可否请您赏光吃饭?"

妇女的脸上绽开了笑容。"我不知道是怎么回事,孩子,"她回答道,"可是刚才走过去的那位穿绿色套装的女士,她央求我把这朵玫瑰插在衣服上。她还说,要是你请我吃饭的话,我就告诉你,她就在街对面那个大饭店里等你。她说这是一种考验!"

梅奈尔小姐的智慧不难理解,也让人钦佩。心灵的本质可以从其对不美的事物的态度中反映出来。

"告诉我你爱什么样的人,"何赛写道,"我就会知道你是什么样的人。"

The Red Rose

By Doug Bell

John Blanchard stood up from the bench, straightened his Army uniform, and studied the crowd of people making their way through Grand Central Station.

He looked for the girl whose heart he knew, but whose face he didn't, the girl with the rose. His interest in her had begun twelve months before in a Florida library. Taking a book off the shelf he soon found himself absorbed, not by the words of the book, but by the notes penciled in the margin. The soft handwriting reflected a thoughtful soul and insightful mind.

In the front of the book, he discovered the previous owner's name, Miss Hollis Maynell. With time and effort he located her address. She lived in New York City. He wrote her a letter introducing himself and inviting her to correspond. The next day he was shipped overseas for service in World War II.

During the next year the two grew to know each other through the mail. Each letter was a seed falling on a fertile heart. A romance was budding. Blanchard requested a photograph, but she refused. She explained: "If your feeling for me has any reality, any honest basis, what I look like won't matter. Suppose I'm beautiful. I'd always be haunted by the feeling that you had been taking a chance on just that, and that kind of love would disgust me. Suppose I'm plain (and you must admit that this is more likely). Then I'd always fear that you were going on writing to me only because you were lonely and had no one else. No, don't ask for my picture. When you come to New York, you shall see me and then you shall make your decision. Remember, both of us are free to stop or to go on after that—whichever we choose..."

When the day finally came for him to return from Europe, they scheduled their first meeting—7:00 p.m. at Grand Central Station, New York.

"You'll recognize me," she wrote, "by the red rose I'll be wearing on my lapel." So, at 7:00 p.m. he was in the station looking for a girl who had filled such a special place in his life for the past twelve months, a girl he had never seen, yet whose written words had been with him and sustained him unfailingly.

I'll let Mr. Blanchard tell you what happened:

A young woman was coming toward me, her figure long and slim. Her golden hair lay back in curls from her delicate ears; her eyes were blue as flowers. Her lips and chin had a gentle firmness, and in her pale green suit she was like springtime come alive.

I started toward her, entirely forgetting to notice that she was not wearing a rose.

As I moved, a small, provocative smile curved her lips. "Going my way, sailor?" she murmured. Almost uncontrollably I made one step closer to her, and then I saw Hollis Maynell. She was standing almost directly behind the girl. A woman well past 40, she had graying hair pinned up under a worn hat.

She was more than a little overweight, her thick-ankled feet thrust into low-heeled shoes.

The girl in the green suit was walking quickly away. I felt as though I was split in two, so keen was my desire to follow her, and yet so deep was my longing for the woman whose spirit had truly companioned me and upheld my own.

And there she stood. Her pale, round face was gentle and sensible, her gray eyes had a warm and kindly glow. I did not hesitate.

My fingers gripped the small worn blue leather copy of the book that was to identify me to her. This would not be love, but it would be something precious, something perhaps even better than love, a friendship for which I had been and must ever be grateful.

I squared my shoulders and saluted and held out the book to the woman, even though while I spoke I felt choked by the bitterness of my disappointment. "I'm Lieutenant John

Blanchard, and you must be Miss Maynell. I am so glad you could meet me; may I take you to dinner?"

The woman's face broadened into a smile. "I don't know what this is about, son," she answered, "but the young lady in the green suit who just went by, she begged me to wear this rose on my coat. And she said if you were to ask me out to dinner, I should go and tell you that she is waiting for you in the big restaurant across the street. She said it was some kind of test!"

It's not difficult to understand and admire Miss Maynell's wisdom. The true nature of a heart is seen in its response to the unattractive.

"Tell me whom you love," Houssaye wrote, "and I will tell you who you are."

银象胸针

埃里克·沃伦和珍妮特·维斯特在同一个办公室工作，埃里克对珍妮特一见钟情。埃里克从前很少和他办公室的女孩子一起出去玩，但现在对珍妮特却另当别论。她不仅人长得很漂亮，谈吐也风趣幽默。他俩在一起吃过几次午餐，并且埃里克很高兴地了解到他们喜好也一样。没过多久，他俩常常共进晚餐，一起看电影、看剧了。几个月后，埃里克意识到他很想娶珍妮特为妻，但他不能肯定她对他的感觉怎样。他们办公室还有一位男生乔治·伯金斯，他时不时地也会和珍妮特一起出去，埃里克希望到时候珍妮特最后会选择他做丈夫，而不是乔治。

埃里克想为珍妮特买一件别致的生日礼物。他走进一家百货商店，却不知道该给她买什么好，他在商店里东逛逛西逛逛，最后到了珠宝部，在这里他开始也没有发现他喜欢的东西，当他正要走开时，突然看到了一个小巧的、大象形状的银制胸针，埃里克立刻感觉到这正是他想为珍妮特买的礼物。

"我可以看看那个吗？"埃里克问店员。

"这枚小银象胸针？"店员问道。

"是的，就是这个，这正是我一直要找的东西。"

"你好眼力啊，挺会选的，这枚胸针非同寻常，是由墨西哥一位著名的能工巧匠制作的，这样的胸针一共也没有几枚。您要我把它装到盒里吗？这个小方盒看起来大小正合适。"

"装吧，请把它装到礼盒里。"

"我可以肯定詹妮特一定会非常高兴。"晚上，埃里克穿戴整齐准备到詹妮特的生日派对去的时候心里想，"她喜欢漂亮的珠宝首饰，而这枚胸针又这么特别。"

在去珍妮特家的路上，埃里克想到了乔治·伯金斯，他知道珍妮特的家人和几个朋友将参加聚会，但他不知道乔治是不是那"几个朋友"中的一个，他坚信乔治的任何礼物将不可能像银象胸针这么特别。

他去詹妮特家的一路上都满心欢喜。来到詹妮特家门口，敲门，开门的是詹妮特，他说："祝你……你……"然后，他停顿了一下才继续说："……生日快乐，詹妮特。"他简直不敢相信他的眼睛：詹妮特的绿色礼服上有一只小象形状的银胸针，和他盒子里的那枚胸针一模一样。那么，他不能送这个礼物了。在詹妮特还没有发现之前，他把礼品盒收了起来，然后进屋去问候詹妮特的父母了。

"你可真早，埃里克先生。"詹妮特的妈妈——威斯特太太说，"其他人还没到呢，请坐吧，我给你拿点什么喝的？"

"现在不想喝，谢谢您，威斯特太太。"埃里克回答道。他现在满脑子都是那枚小银象胸针了。他一定要搞清楚詹妮特是从哪里得到的。是乔治·伯金斯送给她的吗？大概是在办公室送的吧？想到这里，埃里克都不敢想下去，但是，他并不是唯一知道詹妮特喜欢首饰的人，乔治也知道。

詹妮特的妈妈还在跟他说话呢，埃里克知道他应该听着，他不得不暂时忘掉小银象胸针。

"近来工作怎么样，埃里克？"威斯特太太问道，"到年底了，你这几个月一定忙得很。"

"还好,还好,不算太忙,不太忙。"埃里克答道。

"那就好,"威斯特太太说,"请原谅,我得离开几分钟,帮詹妮特在厨房准备几样东西。"

"哦,好的!"埃里克很高兴威斯特太太和詹妮特能离开这个房间。实际上他不想和任何人说话——不管是谈办公室的事还是其他事,他都不想谈。可詹妮特的父亲却还在那儿,他现在开了口。

"你看了今天的晚报吗,埃里克?"威斯特先生问,"里面有一个很有趣的故事……"

詹妮特的父亲滔滔不绝地讲着,但是大多数时间埃里克并没有在听。偶尔他说"是的,温斯特先生"或"我也是这么想的",实际上他并不清楚詹妮特的父亲在谈些什么。他没有忘记那枚银象胸针。埃里克可以肯定他是这个派对上唯一没给詹妮特送礼物的人。他不可能送她已经有的东西。那么,他怎么向詹妮特求婚呢?他不知道该怎么办。

"你对现在的电视怎么看?"威斯特先生现在转换了一下话题,"你不认为那些电视节目应该办得更好吗?"

"您完全正确,威斯特先生。"埃里克答道。詹妮特回到房间里,埃里克很高兴他不用再谈电视了。他告诉詹妮特他很喜欢她礼服上的那枚胸针,正当他准备问这枚胸针的来历时,突然有人敲门。

"一定是我的舅舅和舅母,"詹妮特对埃里克说,"我的邻居,也是我的朋友——玛丽,她今晚也要来。"

"办公室里还有人来吗?"埃里克问。

"没了。"她答道,说着就去门口迎接她的舅舅和舅母去了。

现在,埃里克几乎可以肯定那枚胸针是乔治·伯金斯送的。他一定是白天在办公室给她的。自己可怎么办呢?难道说把礼物落在家里了吗?难道说他从纽约搞到了什么礼物,等到这个星期晚些时候再给她?

几分钟过后,玛丽也到了,于是晚宴开始了,每个人都坐到了餐桌旁。

唯一让埃里克感到安慰的是她这个家庭宴会,乔治·伯金斯没有。末了,詹妮特问埃里克为什么今天晚上话不多。

"今天的晚宴太丰盛了,我吃都来不及呢?"他实在想不出什么别的话来回答。

"非常感谢,埃里克先生,"威斯特太太说,"我很高兴您能喜欢,您还要一些吗?"

埃里克实际上一点儿胃口也没有,但他不好拒绝,他希望他能快点离开餐桌回家,可现在他也不能回家。

到了切生日蛋糕的时候了。"这里有二十一支蜡烛,詹妮特,"威斯特太太说边说边拿出生日蛋糕放到了餐桌上,"你能把它们都吹灭吗?"

"先许个愿,"玛丽对詹妮特说,"吹灭蜡烛前许个愿,说出你最想要的东西。如果蜡烛都灭了,你将实现你的愿望;如果没有全灭,你不会得到。让我们看看你能不能实现你的愿望。"

"我希望我有一枚银象胸针。"詹妮特说着吹灭了所有的蜡烛。

"什么?"埃里克问道,"你刚才说什么?"

"我礼服上的胸针不是我的,是玛丽的。她认为这个胸针很适合我的礼服,借给我戴一个晚上。这是个非同寻常的首饰,玛丽的妈妈去年从墨西哥带给她的。"

埃里克很快抱来了一堆礼物,其中包括他的小方盒子。他简直等不及詹妮特打开礼物盒了。

"现在该你看你的礼物了,詹妮特。"威斯特太太说道。

"是的,"她父亲说,"让我们看一下你是否能实现你的愿望。"

詹妮特一个一个地打开这些礼物的包装。乔治·伯金斯送她一盒纸,他在办公室给她的。她父母送她一台打字机,她舅舅舅母送她几张唱片,玛丽送了她一本书。接着,她打开了那个小方盒子。当她看到那枚胸针时,惊讶地问:"埃里克,你怎么知道我的心愿?这正是我想要的。你真使我高兴,我就知道你的礼物一定会与众不同的。"

詹妮特得偿所愿了,埃里克知道自己也要得偿所愿了,他今晚要向詹妮特求婚。

The Silver Elephant

From the first time he saw her in the office where they both worked, Eric Warren liked Janet West. Eric rarely went out with girls from his office, but Janet was different. She was not only pretty, but extremely interesting to talk to. They had lunch together several times and Eric was pleased to learn that Janet liked the same things he did. Before very long, they were having dinner together, and going to the movies and to the theater. After a few months Eric knew he wanted Janet to be his wife, but he wasn't sure how she felt about him. There was another man in their office, George Perkins, who went out with Janet once in a while. Eric hoped in time he, not George, would be Janet's choice as her husband.

Eric wanted a very unusual gift for Janet's birthday. He walked into a department store not knowing what to get for her. After going from one part of the store to another, he finally came to the jewelry department. At first, he didn't see anything he liked here either, and he was about to leave when he saw a little silver pin in the shape of an elephant. Eric knew immediately that the pin was exactly what he wanted for Janet.

"May I see that?" Eric asked the salesman.

"The little silver elephant?" the salesman asked.

"Yes, that's the one. It's just what I've been looking for."

"You've made a good choice. This piece of jewelry is very unusual. It was made in Mexico by a man who is well-known for his fine work in silver. There are only a few others like it. Would you like me to put it in a box? This small square box looks about the right size."

"Yes, please put it in a gift box."

"I'm certain Janet's going to be very pleased," Eric thought that evening as he got dressed to go to Janet's birthday party. "She likes fine jewelry and this pin is very unusual."

On the way to Janet's house, Eric thought about George Perkins. He knew that Janet's family and a few friends would be at the party. He didn't know if George was one of the "few friends". He was fairly sure George's gift wouldn't be anything as unusual as the silver elephant.

Eric was happy as he walked to Janet's house. When she opened the door he said, "Happy…" and then stopped talking for a moment before going on, "…birthday, Janet." He just couldn't believe what he saw. There on Janet's green dress was a little silver elephant pin. It was exactly the same as the one in his gift box. He couldn't give it to her now. He put the little square box away before Janet could see it and went in the house to say hello to Janet's mother and father.

"You're early, Eric," Mrs. West said. "None of the others are here yet. Please sit down. Can I get you something to drink?"

"Not now, thanks, Mrs. West," Eric answered. All he could think about was the little silver elephant. He had to know where Janet had gotten it. Could George Perkins possibly have given it to her? At the office perhaps? Eric didn't want to believe this, but he wasn't the only one who knew Janet liked jewelry. George knew it, too.

Janet's mother was still talking and Eric knew he should be listening to her. He had to forget about the little pin for a moment.

"How are things at the office, Eric?" Mrs. West was saying. "I understand you've been very busy during the last few months."

"Fine—just fine—not too busy, no," Eric said.

"That's good," Mrs. West answered. "Would you excuse us for a few minutes? I have to help Janet prepare a few things in the kitchen."

"Oh—yes." Eric was glad to see Mrs. West and Janet leave the room. He really didn't want to talk to anyone—not about the office or about anything else. But Janet's father was still there, and now he was talking.

"Have you seen this evening's newspaper yet, Eric?" Mr.

West asked. "There is a good story about..."

Janet's father went on talking, but most of the time Eric wasn't listening. Occasionally he would say, "You're right, Mr. West," or "I think so, too," but he really wasn't sure what Janet's father was talking about. He couldn't forget the elephant pin. Eric was positive he would be the only person at the party who wouldn't have a gift for Janet. But he couldn't give her something that she already had. How could he ask Janet to be his wife now? He didn't know what to do.

"What do you think about television?" Mr. West was talking about a different subject now. "Don't you think the programs could be better?"

"You're absolutely right, Mr. West," Eric answered. Janet came back in the room and Eric was glad he didn't have to say any more about television. He started to tell Janet he liked the pin on her dress, thinking that he might learn where it came from. But just at this moment someone came to the door.

"It must be my aunt and uncle," Janet told Eric. "My friend, Marie, who lives next door, will be with us, too."

"Isn't anyone else from the office coming?" Eric asked.

"No," she answered, then went to meet her aunt and uncle at the door.

Now Eric was almost certain the pin was from George. He must have given it the office during the day. What should he do?

Should he say he had left his gift at home? Should he say he was getting something in New York and would give it to her later in the week?

Marie came in a few minutes later, and everyone sat down to have dinner.

The only good thing Eric could think about was that he was at the family dinner party and George was not.

Finally Janet asked him why he wasn't talking very much.

"I'm too busy eating this very good dinner," he answered. He couldn't think of anything else to say.

"Thank you, Eric," Mrs. West said. "I'm very glad you like it. Won't you have some more?"

Eric didn't really want to eat anything, but he wasn't able to say no. He wished he could leave the table and go home, but he couldn't do that, either.

Finally it was time for the birthday cake. "There are twenty-one candles on the cake, Janet," Mrs. West said as she brought the cake in and put it on the dinner table. "Do you think you can blow them all out?"

"Make a wish first," Marie said to Janet. "Wish for something that you want very much before you blow out the candles. If all the candles go out, you will get your wish. If not, then you won't. Let's see if you'll get your wish."

"I wish I had a silver elephant pin," Janet said and she blew out all the candles.

"What?" said Eric. "What did you say?"

"The pin on my dress isn't mine. It's Marie's. She thought it looked good on this dress and she said I could have it for this evening. It's a very unusual piece of jewelry. Marie's mother got it when she was in Mexico last year."

Eric quickly put his little square box with the other gifts. He couldn't wait for Janet to open it.

"It's time to open your gifts now, Janet," Mrs. West said.

"Yes," said her father. "Let's see if you get your wish."

Janet opened all her gifts. She got a box of writing paper from George. He had given it to her at the office. Her parents gave her a typewriter, her aunt and uncle gave her some phonograph records, and Marie gave her a book. Then Janet opened the little square box. When she saw the pin, she said, "Eric, how could you possibly have known? It's exactly what I want. You've made me very happy. I knew that your gift would be very unusual."

Janet got her wish, and now Eric was sure he would get his wish, too. Tonight he would ask Janet to be his wife.

生死相随

那天，天气晴朗。一对约莫七十多岁的老夫妇走进了一家律师事务所，很明显是来办离婚手续的。律师大惑不解，直到跟他们聊过以后，才了解了事情的缘由。

这老两口吵吵闹闹过了四十多年，似乎一切都格格不入。可是，就因为害怕离婚给孩子的成长带来不良影响，为了孩子，一直拖延着，将就着过。如今，孩子们都长大成人了，也有他们各自的家庭了，两位老人再没有顾虑了。他们想做的只是过上各自向往的生活，不再受不幸婚姻的束缚，所以两个人同意协议离婚。

准备离婚材料的过程令律师备受煎熬。他怎么也想不明白70岁的老人，结婚40年了怎么还要分道扬镳呢？

签协议时，妻子对丈夫说："我是真的爱你，可是我真的爱不动了。对不起！"

"好的，我懂。"丈夫说。看到这一幕，律师提议一起吃晚饭，就他们三个人。妻子想了想，去吧，以后还是朋友呢。

餐桌上，大家都沉默不语，气氛令人尴尬。

第一道菜是烤鸡，菜刚端上来，老头就立刻给老太太夹了个鸡腿。"吃这个，你的最爱。"

看到这一幕，律师想事情也许会有转机。但是老太太却皱起了眉，说道："每次都这样，你总是自以为是，却从来不考虑我的感受。你不知道吧，我其实不喜欢鸡腿。"

可她不知道，这些年来丈夫花尽心思取悦于她。她不知道，鸡腿是丈夫的最爱。

他不知道，她觉得他根本不懂她。他不知道，她不喜欢鸡腿，尽管他只想把最好的给她。

那夜，两个人辗转反侧，久久不能入睡。几小时后，老头再也忍不住了，他知道还爱着她，离不开她，想要她回心转意，想告诉她，他心存愧疚，他一直想告诉她"我爱你"。

他拿起电话，按下号码，铃声响个不停，但另一边却没人接。尽管对方不接他的电话，他还是一直不停地在按着重拨键。

那边，她也不好过。她不明白，一起生活这么多年，他怎么还是一点儿都不懂她。她还是很爱他，只是再也爱不动了。电话响了，知道是他，她没接。"现在谈论还有什么意思呢？我和你的感情已经结束了。当初，第一次提出离婚的人是我，那我现在也得保持这种现状。要不然，你会说我反悔，那我岂不是很丢脸。对，对，就这样下去。"老夫人心想道。电话铃声仍然在响，她于是索性把电话线拔掉了。

她不记得，他有心脏病。

第二天早上，老夫人得知她丈夫昨晚已去世的消息。她径直冲进他的公寓，发现丈夫的尸体躺在沙发上，手里仍然拿着电话。那天晚上，当她的丈夫试图接通她的电话时，心脏病突然发作，他就这样离开了她。

虽然她伤心欲绝，可是遗物还是要整理的。她仔仔细细检查抽屉时，发现一份保单，保险日期从他们结婚之日起算起，保险受益人是她。跟文件一起还有一份遗嘱，内容如下：

献给我最亲爱的妻子：当你读着这封遗嘱的时候，我确信我已不在你的身边了。我为你买了这份保险。虽然金额总数才区区100万美元，但我希望它能帮助我继续履行我们结婚时我所许下的诺言：照顾你一生一世。我不能再陪你一起度过你的余生，但我希望保险金额里的钱能够帮助我实现照顾你后半生生活的愿望，就可以像我还在的时候那样照顾你。我同时也想让你知道，我会一直在你左右，在你的身边。我爱你！

泪如雨下。

当你爱着别人的时候，务必要让他们知道，因为你永远不知道下一分钟将会发生什么事。学会一起共创生活，学会相亲相爱，不论他们是谁，跟你是什么关系……

Life Together

One fine day, an old couple around the age of 70, walks into a lawyer's office. Apparently, they are there to file a divorce. Lawyer was very puzzled, after having a chat with them, he got their story.

This couple had been quarreling all their 40 over years of marriage nothing ever seems to go right. They hang on because of their children, afraid that it might affect their up-bringing. Now, all their children have already grown up, have their own family, there's nothing else the old couple have to worry about, all they wanted is to lead their own life free from all these years of unhappiness from their marriage, so both agree on a divorce.

Lawyer was having a hard time trying to get the papers done, because he felt that after 40 years of marriage at the age of 70, he couldn't understand why the old couple would still wants a divorce.

While they were signing the papers, the wife told the husband. "I really love you, but I really can't carry on anymore, I'm sorry."

"It's OK, I understand." said the husband. Looking at this, the lawyer suggested a dinner together, just three of them, wife thought, why not, since they are still going be friends.

At the dining table, there was a silence of awkwardness.

The first dish was roasted chicken, immediately, the old man took the drumstick for the old lady. "Take this, it's your favorite."

Looking at this, the lawyer thought maybe there's still a chance, but the wife was frowning when she answered. "This is always the problem, you always think so highly of yourself, never thought about how I feel, don't you know that I hate drumsticks?"

Little did she know that, over the years, the husband have been trying all ways to please her, little did she know that drumsticks was the husband's favorite.

Little did he know that she never thought he understand her at all, little did he know that she hates drumsticks even though all he wants is the best for her.

That night, both of them couldn't sleep, toss and turn, toss and turn. After hours, the old man couldn't take it anymore, he knows that he still loves her, and he can't carry on life without her, he wants her back, he wants to tell her, he is sorry, he wanted to tell her, "I love you".

He picks up the phone, started dialing her number. Ringing

never stops. He never stop dialing.

On the other side, she was sad, she couldn't understand how come after all these years, he still doesn't understand her at all, she loves him a lot, but she just can't take it any more. Phone's ringing, she refuses to answer knowing that it's him. "What's the point of talking now that it's over. I have asked for it and now. I want to keep it this way, if not I will lose face." She thought. Phone still ringing. She has decided to pull out the cord.

Little did she remember, he had heart problems.

The next day, she received news that he had passed away. She rushed down to his apartment, saw his body, lying on the couch still holding on to the phone. He had a heart attack when he was still trying to get thru her phone line.

As sad as she could be. She will have to clear his belongings. When she was looking thru the drawers, she saw this insurance policy, dated from the day they got married, beneficiary is her. Together in that file there's this note.

To my dearest wife, by the time you are reading this, I'm sure I'm no longer around, I bought this policy for you, though the amount is only $100k, I hope it will be able to help me continue my promise that I have made when we got married, I might not be around anymore, I want this amount of money to continue taking care of you, just like the way

I will if I could have live longer. I want you to know I will always be around, by your side. I love you.

Tears flowed like river.

When you love someone, let them know... You never know what will happen the next minute... Learn to build a life together... Learn to love each other... For who they are... Not what they are...

一封神奇的情书

从前,一个小伙子深深地爱一位姑娘,但姑娘的父亲却不喜欢他,也不希望他们的爱情发展下去。小伙子很想给姑娘写封情书,然而他知道姑娘的父亲会抢先看,于是他给姑娘写了这样一封信:

我对你表达过的爱
已经消逝。相反,我对你的厌恶
与日俱增。下次我看到你时
我甚至不喜欢你的那副样子。
我只想做的一件事就是
转过头去不看你,你永远不要指望我会
跟你结婚。我们的最近一次谈话
是那么枯燥乏味,因此你不要想
让我渴望与你再见。
假如我们结婚,
我深信我将
生活得非常艰难,我也绝对不会
愉快地和你生活在一起,我要把我的心
奉献出来,但决不是

奉献给你。没有人能比你更

苛刻和自私,谁都比你更

关心我体贴我。

我真挚地要你明白,

我讲的是真话,请你帮我一个忙

结束我们之间的关系,别试图

答复此信,你的信总是充满了

让我不愉快的内容,你并没有

真正关心我的心意。再见,请相信

我不再喜欢你了,请你不要以为

我仍然爱着你!

  姑娘的父亲看了这封信以后如释重负,放心地把信给了姑娘。姑娘仔仔细细地看了信,也非常快乐,知道她的小伙子依然深爱着她。你知道为什么吗?其实,她读第一遍时非常忧伤,可是她又读了几遍以后,终于,她明白了该怎么读。只能隔一行一读,也就是第一行、第三行、第五行……以此类推,读到信的结尾。

An Ingenious Letter

There once lived a lad who was deeply in love with a girl, but disliked by the girl's father, who didn't want to see any further development of their love. The lad was eager to write to the girl, yet he was quite sure that the father would read it first. So he wrote such a letter to the girl:

My love for you I once expressed
no longer lasts, instead, my distaste for you
is growing with each passing day. Next time I see you,
I even won't like that look of yours.
I'll do nothing but
look away from you. You can never expect I'll
marry you. The last chat we had
was so dull and dry that you shouldn't think it
make me eager to see you again.
If we get married,
I firmly believe I'll
live a hard life, I can never

live happily with you, I'll devote myself

but not

to you. No one else is more

harsh and selfish and less

solicitous and considerate than you.

I sincerely want to let you know

what I said is true. Please do me a favor by

ending our relations and refrain from

writing me a reply. Your letter is always full of

things which displease me. You have no

sincere care for me. So long! Please believe

I don't love you any longer. Don't think

I still have a love of you!

Having read the letter, the father felt relieved and gave it to his daughter with a light heart. The girl also felt quite pleased after she read it carefully, her lad still had a deep love for her. Do you know why? In fact, she felt very sad when she read the letter for the first time. But she read it for a few more times and, at last, she found the key—only every other line should be read, that is the first line, the third, the fifth…and so on to the end.

有情人

几年前的一个寒冷的日子,我在街上捡到了一个钱包。里面没有任何能够证明身份的证件,只有三美元和一张揉皱的信,看起来好像已经随身携带了很多年了。

上面唯一能够辨认出的是破旧信封上的回信地址。我打开信,发现是在 1924 年写的,差不多就是 60 年前。我仔仔细细读了一遍,希望能够找到任何识别钱包主人的线索。

这是一封女生写给男生的绝交信。写信人娟秀的字迹告诉一个叫迈克尔的收信人,她的母亲禁止她再和他见面。但是,她将永远爱他。落款署名是汉纳。

这封信写得非常优美,但其中除了迈克尔这个名字之外,没有任何能够识别失主的东西。我询问一下咨询处,接线员也许能够找到信封上地址的电话号码。

"接线员,您好,我有一个不同寻常的请求。我捡到一个钱包,希望能找到失主。钱包里有一封信,上面有地址,您能否帮我找到这个地址的电话号码?"

接线员把电话转给主管。主管说虽然找到了这个地址的电话,但是她不能把号码给我。不过,她可以替我打电话解释一下情况。如果对方同意谈话,她将和我联系。一分钟以后,她回到电话旁告诉我:"有位女士要和你谈话。"

我问那位女士是否认识一个名叫汉纳的人。

"哦,当然了,我们这幢房子就是三十年前从汉纳手里买的。"

我问道:"那你知道她们现在住哪儿吗?"

"几年前,汉纳把她母亲送到了养老院。也许你可以从那里得到些帮助,顺藤摸瓜找到汉纳。"

这位女士把养老院的名称给了我。我打过去电话,了解到汉纳的母亲已经去世。接电话的女士又给了我一个地址。她说汉纳可能会在那里。

我拨通了电话,接电话的女士解释说汉纳本人现在也住在养老院。她把电话号码给了我。我打过去,对方告诉我:"是的,汉纳在我们这里。"

我询问能否去探望她。此时将近晚上 10 点了。主任说汉纳可能已经睡了。"不过,如果你想碰碰运气的话,她可能还在活动室看电视呢。"

主任和保安在养老院的门口迎接我。我们一起去了三楼,见到了护士。她告诉我们说汉纳确实还在看电视。

我们走进了活动室。汉纳是一位非常慈祥的银发老人,她笑容温暖,目光和蔼。我把捡到钱包的事情告诉了她,并拿出了那封信。在看到信的那一瞬间,她深深地吸了一口气,说:"年轻人,这封信是我最后一次与迈克尔联系。"她有好一会儿,她转过头去望着别处,若有所思地说:"我非常爱他。但当时我只有十六岁,妈妈认为我太年轻了。他那么英俊,就像扮演 007 的演员肖恩·康奈利似的。"

我们都笑了。这时,主任走了出去,屋子里只剩下我们两个人。她说道:"是的,他叫迈克尔·戈尔茨坦。如果你找到他,请告诉他,我依然会经常想起他。我一直没有结婚。"她微笑着，泪水从眼眶涌出。"我想没有人能够配得上迈克尔……"

我谢过汉纳，跟她道了别。然后乘电梯到了一楼。在门口的时候，保安问我："那位老妇人对您有什么帮助吗？"

我说她给了我一些提示。"至少，我知道了失主的名字。不过，我可能一时无法继续追查下去了。"我跟他说我一整天都在找钱包的主人。

说话的时候，我拿出了那个镶着红短花边的黄皮钱包给保安看。他凑到跟前看了一眼，说："嘿，我知道这是谁的。这是戈尔茨坦先生的，他经常弄丢，我在大厅至少捡到过三次。"

我问道："戈尔茨坦先生是谁？""他是住在八楼的一位老人。这肯定是迈克尔·戈尔茨坦的钱包。他常常出去散步。"

我谢过保安，回到主任的办公室，告诉了他保安的话。他陪我来到了八层。我企望戈尔茨坦先生还没有睡觉。

护士说："我想他一定还在活动室。他喜欢在晚上读书……是一位非常可爱的老人。"

我们来到唯一一间还亮着灯的房间，有位老人在那里看书。主任问他是否丢了钱包。迈克尔·戈尔茨坦找了找，翻了翻后裤兜，然后说："天哪！竟然丢了。"

"这位好心的先生捡到了一个钱包。是你的吗？"

他一看到钱包就如释重负地笑了，说道："是的。就是它。一定是今天下午丢的。我要给您报酬。"

"哦，不要，谢谢你。"我说道，"不过，我要告诉您一件事情。我读了里面的信，希望能找到钱包的主人。"

他脸上的笑容顿时消失了:"你读过那封信?"

"我不仅读过,而且还知道汉纳在哪儿。"

他顿时脸色苍白:"汉纳?你知道汉纳在哪儿?她过得怎么样?她还像年轻时那么美丽吗?"

我迟疑着。

迈克尔催促着说:"请告诉我!"

"她很好,和你认识她时一样美丽。"

"您能告诉我她在哪儿吗?我想明天给她打电话。"

他抓住我的手说:"您一定知道些什么。在我收到信的那一天,我的生活就完结了。我从未结婚。我想我一直爱着她。"

我说:"迈克尔,跟我来。"我们三个人乘电梯来到了三层。我们走进活动室,发现汉纳还在看电视。主任过去告诉她说:"汉纳,你认识这个人吗?"

迈克尔和我站在门口等待她的回答。

她扶了一下眼镜,看了一会儿,但是没有说话。

"汉纳,我是迈克尔,迈克尔·戈尔茨坦,你不记得了吗?"

"迈克尔?迈克尔?真的是你吗?"

他慢慢走到她的旁边,她站了起来,他们拥抱在一起,然后坐在长沙发上,双手紧紧地握在一起,开始说话。主任和我走了出去,我们两个人都已热泪盈眶。

我乐观地说:"真是天意啊。天意如此就该如此。"

三个星期后,我接到主任的电话,他问:"这周日能抽出时间参加婚礼吗?"他没等我回答就接着说道:"是这样,迈克尔和汉纳要终成眷属了。"

那是一场非常感人的婚礼，养老院所有的人都参加了。汉纳穿着一身米色礼服，看起来非常美丽。迈克尔穿着深蓝色的西装，显得非常高大。养老院为他们提供了单独的房间，如果您想看看像十几岁一样的76岁的新娘和78岁的新郎的话，就来看看这一对吧。

这个持续了近60年的爱情故事终于有了个大团圆的完美结局。

Letter in the Wallet

It was a freezing day, a few years ago, when I stumbled on a wallet in the street. There was no identification inside. Just three dollars, and a crumpled letter that looked as if it had been carried around for years.

The only thing legible on the torn envelope was the return address. I opened the letter and saw that it had been written in 1924—almost 60 years ago. I read it carefully, hoping to find some clue to the identity of the wallet's owner.

It was a "Dear John" letter. The writer, in a delicate script, told the recipient, whose name was Michael, that her mother forbade her to see him again. Nevertheless, she would always love him. It was signed Hannah.

It was a beautiful letter. But there was no way, beyond the name Michael, to identify the owner. Perhaps if I called information the operator could find the phone number for the address shown on the envelope.

"Operator, this is an unusual request. I'm trying to find the owner of a wallet I found. Is there any way you could tell me the phone number for an address that was on a letter in the wallet?"

The operator gave me her supervisor, who said there was a phone listed at the address, but that she could not give me the number. However, she would call and explain the situation. Then, if the party wanted to talk, she would connect me. I waited a minute and she came back on the line. "I have a woman who will speak with you."

I asked the woman if she knew a Hannah.

"Oh, of course! We bought this house from Hannah's family thirty years ago."

"Would you know where they could be located now?" I asked.

"Hannah had to place her mother in a nursing home years ago. Maybe the home could help you track down the daughter."

The woman gave me the name of the nursing home. I called and found out that Hannah's mother had died. The woman I spoke with gave me an address where she thought Hannah could be reached.

I phoned. The woman who answered explained that Hannah herself was now living in a nursing home. She gave me the number. I called and was told, "Yes, Hannah is with us."

I asked if I could stop by to see her. It was almost 10 p.m. The director said Hannah might be asleep. "But if you want to take a chance, maybe she's in the day room watching television."

The director and a guard greeted me at the door of the nursing home. We went up to the third floor and saw the nurse, who told us that Hannah was indeed watching TV.

We entered the day room. Hannah was a sweet, silver-haired old-timer with a warm smile and friendly eyes. I told her about finding the wallet and showed her the letter. The second she saw it, she took a deep breath. "Young man," she said, "this letter was the last contact I had with Michael." She looked away for a moment, then said pensively, "I loved him very much. But I was only sixteen and my mother felt I was too young. He was so handsome. You know, like Sean Connery, the actor."

We both laughed. The director then left us alone. "Yes, Michael Goldstein was his name. If you find him, tell him I still think of him often. I never did marry," she said, smiling through tears that welled up in her eyes. "I guess no one ever matched up to Michael…"

I thanked Hannah, said good-by and took the elevator to the first floor. As I stood at the door, the guard asked, "Was the old lady able to help you?"

I told him she had given me a lead. "At least I have a last name. But I probably won't pursue it further for a while." I explained that I had spent almost the whole day trying to find the wallet's owner.

While we talked, I pulled out the brown-leather case with

its red-lanyard lacing and showed it to the guard. He looked at it closely and said, "Hey, I'd know that anywhere. That's Mr. Goldstein's. He's always losing it. I found it in the hall at least three times."

"Who's Mr. Goldstein?" I asked. "He's one of the old-timers on the eighth floor. That's Mike Goldstein's wallet, for sure. He goes out for a walk quite often."

I thanked the guard and ran back to the director's office to tell him what the guard had said. He accompanied me to the eighth floor. I prayed that Mr. Goldstein would be up.

"I think he's still in the day room," the nurse said. "He likes to read at night…a darling old man."

We went to the only room that had lights on, and there was a man reading a book. The director asked him if he had lost his wallet? Michael Goldstein looked up, felt his back pocket and then said, "Goodness, it is missing."

"This kind gentleman found a wallet. Could it be yours?"

The second he saw it, he smiled with relief. "Yes," he said, "that's it. Must have dropped it this afternoon. I want to give you a reward."

"Oh, no, thank you," I said. "But I have to tell you something. I read the letter in the hope of finding out who owned the wallet."

The smile on his face disappeared. "You read that letter?"

"Not only did I read it, I think I know where Hannah is."

He grew pale. "Hannah? You know where she is? How is she? Is she still as pretty as she was?"

I hesitated.

"Please tell me!" Michael urged.

"She's fine, and just as pretty as when you knew her."

"Could you tell me where she is? I want to call her tomorrow."

He grabbed my hand and said, "You know something? When that letter came, my life ended. I never married. I guess I've always loved her."

"Michael," I said. "Come with me." The three of us took the elevator to the third floor. We walked toward the day room where Hannah was sitting, still watching TV. The director went over to her. "Hannah," he said softly. "Do you know this man?"

Michael and I stood waiting in the doorway.

She adjusted her glasses, looked for a moment, but didn't say a word.

"Hannah, it's Michael. Michael Goldstein. Do you remember?"

"Michael? Michael? It's you!"

He walked slowly to her side. She stood and they embraced. Then the two of them sat on a couch, held hands and started to talk. The director and I walked out, both of us crying.

"See how the good Lord works," I said philosophically. "If it's meant to be. it will be."

Three weeks later, I got a call from the director who asked. "Can you break away on Sunday to attend a wedding?" He didn't wait for an answer. "Yup(=yes), Michael and Hannah are going to tie the knot!"

It was a lovely wedding, with all the people at the nursing home joining in the celebration. Hannah wore a beige dress and looked beautiful. Michael wore a dark blue suit and stood tall. The home gave them their own room, and if you ever wanted to see a 76-year-old bride and a 78-year-old groom acting like two teenagers, you had to see this couple.

A perfect ending for a love affair that had lasted nearly 60 years.

天使何所似

天使何所似?

天使恰似——

那个昨天那个把钱包物归原主的瘦小干枯的老夫人。

那个告诉你,当你美目流盼,微微一笑很倾城的出租车司机。

那个让你看到简单事物中蕴含奇迹的小孩儿。

那个主动提出跟你分享午餐的穷人。

那个让你看到心若在梦就在的富人。

那个你迷路时碰巧过来指点迷津的陌生人。

那个你以为自己已经心如死灰时,让你死灰复燃的朋友。

天使无处不在,他们高矮胖瘦不同,姿态万千,老中青不拘,黑黄白不限。

有的雀斑点点,有的笑靥深深,有的满脸皱纹,有的皓质呈露。

他们可能装扮成你的朋友、敌人、老师、学生、恋人,抑或傻瓜。

他们不板着面孔对待生活,因而身轻如燕。

他们不会留下地址,因为他们不求报答。

他们的球鞋上有丝网般的羽翼,他们跟干洗店有约在先。

选择合上双眼,天使很难发现;选择睁大双眼,天使会在任何地方出现。

What do Angels Look Like

What do angels look like?

They are—

Like the little old lady who returned your wallet yesterday.

Like the taxi driver who told you that your eyes light up the world when you smile.

Like the small child who showed you the wonder in simple things.

Like the poor man who offered to share his lunch with you.

Like the rich man who showed you it really is all possible, if only you believe.

Like the stranger who just happened to come along, when you had lost your way.

Like the friend who touched your heart, when you didn't think you had one left to touch.

Angels come in all sizes and shapes, all ages and skin types.

Some with freckles, some with dimples, some with wrinkles, some without.

They come disguised as friends, enemies, teachers,

students, lovers and fools.

They don't take life too seriously, they travel light.

They leave no forwarding address, they ask for nothing in return.

They wear sneakers with gossamer wings, they get a deal on dry cleaning.

They are hard to find when your eyes are closed, but they are everywhere you look when you choose to see.

现在是春天

一天,一位盲人坐在建筑物的台阶上,他的脚边放着一个牌子,那上面写着:"我是盲人,请帮帮我。"

一个有创意的广告员走到那位盲人身旁,他发现盲人的帽子里只有屈指可数的几个硬币。他往帽子里投了几个硬币,接下来,没有征得盲人的同意就拿起牌子,将牌子翻过来,写了一些新的信息。然后,他将牌子放到盲人的脚下就离开了。

那天下午的晚些时候,那位广告员回家经过盲人那里,发现盲人帽子里的纸币和硬币都快装满了。盲人听出了他的脚步声,问广告员是不是把他的牌子的内容换了?盲人还想知道广告员往牌子上写了什么。

盲人不知道牌子的背面上改写成了这样的字样:"现在是春天,我却看不见。"

It's Spring

One day, there was a blind man sitting on the steps of a building with a sign by his feet, that reads: "I am blind, please help."

A creative publicist was walking by the blind man and stopped to observe that the man only had a few coins in his hat. He put a few of his own coins in the hat, and without stopping to ask for permission, took the sign, turned it around, and wrote a new message. He then placed the sign by the feet of the blind man, and left.

Later that afternoon the creative publicist returned by the blind man and noticed that his hat was almost completely full of bills and coins. The blind man recognized his footsteps and asked if it was him who had changed his sign? He also wanted to know what the man wrote on it.

The blind man didn't know that his new sign reads as this: "It's spring now, but I can't see it."

爱情永不失明

当这个手持白杖的年轻漂亮的女人小心翼翼地登上公共汽车的踏板时，车上的乘客都向她投去怜悯的目光。她向司机付了车费之后，双手摸索着座位，从过道上走过，然后坐好，把公文包放在膝盖上，手杖靠着腿。

34岁的苏珊失明已有一年了。一起医疗事故夺去了她的视力，她顿时陷入黑暗之中，内心充满愤怒、沮丧，还有顾影自怜，她可以依靠的只有她的丈夫马克了。

马克是一名空军军官，他全心全意爱着苏珊。在苏珊刚刚失明的那些日子里，他眼睁睁地看着妻子陷入绝望，心中暗下决心，要帮助妻子重拾力量和信心，再次独立起来。

苏珊终于愿意重返工作岗位了。可她怎么去上班呢？以前都是乘公交车去的，但是她现在很害怕，自己一个人不敢在城里转。于是马克自告奋勇地每天开车接送，尽管两个人的工作地点在城市相反方向的尽头。

开始，这让苏珊备感安慰，也满足了马克要保护失明的妻子事无巨细都没有危险的心理需求。可是，没过多久，马克就意识到这样的安排不起作用。他暗自承认，苏珊还是需要自己再像失明以前一样自己坐公共汽车才行。可是，她还那么脆弱，那么愤怒——她会有什么样的反应呢?

正如他所预料的那样,苏珊一想到自己坐公共汽车就感到恐怖。"我瞎啦!"她痛苦地回答。"我怎么知道方向呢?我感觉你在抛弃我。"

听到这些话,马克的心都碎了,可是他知道应该做什么。

他答应苏珊自己每天早晚都会陪她坐公共汽车,直到她可以自己坐车为止。

这就是事情的原委。整整两个星期,马克每天都一身戎装,陪着苏珊一起上下班,教她怎么凭借视觉以外的其他感觉,尤其是听觉,来判断她所处的位置,以及如何适应新的环境。他还帮她与司机交朋友,这样司机能留意她,还能给她留个座位。

最后,苏珊感觉自己已经准备好了,决定试试独自坐车上班。星期一上午,临行前,她紧紧地拥抱着她的丈夫,前段时间陪她坐公共汽车的人——马克,心存感激,热泪盈眶,感谢他的忠诚,他的耐心,还有他的爱。她向他道了别,他们第一次朝着不同的方向走去。

周一、周二、周三、周四……每天她的独行之旅都很顺利,苏珊的感觉从来没有这么好过。她成功了!她真的能一个人去上班了。

周五早上,苏珊照常乘公共汽车去上班。就要下车了,司机说:"小姐,我真羡慕你啊。"

苏珊都不敢肯定司机是不是在跟自己说话,说到底,一个一年来挣扎着寻找活下去的勇气的瞎眼女人有什么可羡慕的?于是,她好奇地问司机,"你为什么说羡慕我呢?"

司机回答:"被用心照顾和保护的感觉一定非常棒吧?"

苏珊搞不懂司机在说什么,就又问了一次:"您指的是什么?"

司机答道,"是这样的,过去的这一星期,每天早上都有一个仪表堂堂穿着军装的男士一直站在拐弯处看着你下车，看着你安全地穿过街道，又看着你走进办公楼，他向你飞一个吻，冲你简单地行个礼，然后才动身离去。你真是个幸运的女士啊！"

苏珊顿时泪如泉涌，因为她的眼睛虽然看不见他，但她却一直都能感觉到他的存在。她是如此的幸运，因为马克给了她比视力更珍贵的礼物，一份她不需要看就能体会到的礼物——这就是爱的礼物，它能给黑暗带来光明。

A Gift of Love

The passengers on the bus watched sympathetically as the attractive young woman with the white cane made her way carefully up the steps. She paid the driver and, using her hands to feel the location of the seats, walked down the aisle and found the seat he'd told her was empty. Then she settled in, placed her briefcase on her lap and rested her cane against her leg.

It had been a year since Susan, 34, became blind. Due to a medical misdiagnosis she had been rendered sightless, and she was suddenly thrown into a world of darkness, anger, frustration and self pity. And all she had to cling to was her husband, Mark.

Mark was an Air Force officer and he loved Susan with all his heart. When she first lost her sight, he watched her sink into despair and was determined to help his wife gain the strength and confidence she needed to become independent again.

Finally, Susan felt ready to return to her job, but how would she get there? She used to take the bus, but was now too frightened to get around the city by herself. Mark volunteered to drive her to work each day, even though they worked at opposite ends of the city.

At first, this comforted Susan, and fulfilled Mark's need to protect his sightless wife who was so insecure about performing the slightest task. Soon, however, Mark realized the arrangement wasn't working. Susan is going to have to start taking the bus again, he admitted to himself. But she was still so fragile, so angry—how would she react?

Just as he predicted, Susan was horrified at the idea of taking the bus again. "I'm blind!" she responded bitterly. "How am I supposed to know where I am going? I feel like you're abandoning me."

Mark's heart broke to hear these words, but he knew what had to be done.

He promised Susan that each morning and evening he would ride the bus with her, for as long as it took, until she got the hang of it.

And that is exactly what happened. For two solid weeks, Mark, military uniform and all, accompanied Susan to and from work each day. He taught her how to rely on her other senses, specifically her hearing, to determine where she was and how to adapt her new environment. He helped her befriend the bus drivers who could watch out for her, and save her a seat.

Finally, Susan decided that she was ready to try the trip on her own. Monday morning arrived, and before she left, she threw her arms around Mark, her temporary bus riding companion, her husband, and her best friend. Her eyes filled with tears of gratitude for his loyalty, his patience, and his love. She said good-bye, and for the first time, they went their separate ways.

Monday, Tuesday, Wednesday, Thursday... Each day on her own went perfectly, and Susan had never felt better. She was doing it! She was going to work all by herself.

On Friday morning, Susan took the bus to work as usual. As she was paying the fare to exit the bus, the driver said, "Lady, I sure do envy you."

Susan wasn't sure if the driver was speaking to her or not. After all, who on earth would ever envy a blind woman who had struggled just to find the courage to live for the past year? Curious, she asked the driver, "Why do you say that you envy me?"

The driver responded, "It must feel good to be taken care of and protected like you are."

Susan had no idea what the driver was talking about, and again asked, "What do you mean?"

The driver answered, "You know, every morning for the past week, a fine looking gentleman in a military uniform has been standing across the corner watching you as you get off the bus. He makes sure you cross the street safely and he watches until you enter your office building. Then he blows you a kiss, gives you a little salute and walks away. You are one lucky lady."

Tears of happiness poured down Susan's cheeks. For although she couldn't physically see him, she had always felt Mark's presence. She was lucky, so lucky, for he had given her a gift more powerful than sight, a gift she didn't need to see to believe—the gift of love that can bring light where there is darkness.

情路崎岖

由于我的工作地点在联合车站的行李寄存处,所以每一个上楼的人我都能看见。

三年多以前,哈里曾经来过这里,曾经站在楼梯口等待 9 点 5 分到达的火车旅客。

我还记得那第一晚见到哈里时的情景。那时的他不过是一个身体瘦削、神情焦虑的孩子。他打扮得整整齐齐的,我知道他是在等女朋友,我还知道在她到达二十分钟之后他们就要结婚。

旅客们出来了,我得忙碌起来。等到 9 点 18 分的那趟车快到的时候我才再往楼梯方向看去,我吃惊地发现那个年轻人还在那里。

她也没乘 9 点 18 分的那趟车来,9 点 40 分的车上也没她。等 10 点 2 分那趟车的旅客全都到达并离开后,哈里显得很失望。很快他走近我的窗口,我大声问他她长什么模样。

"她个子小,皮肤黑,"他说道,"19 岁。走路的样子很敏捷。她的脸上,"他想了一会儿,说,"表情丰富。我的意思是说她会生气,但从不会生气太久。她的眉心处有一个小点儿。她有一件褐色毛皮大衣,不过可能没穿着。"

我想不起来见过的旅客里有这样长相的人。

他把他收到的电报给我看:星期四到。车站接我。爱爱爱爱。——

梅。电报寄自内布拉斯加州的奥马哈市。

"呃,"我最后说道,"你干吗不往家里打个电话?如果她比你先到这里,她可能已给你家打过电话了。"

他失望地看了我一眼。"我到城里才两天。我们打算见面之后开车去南方,我在那儿找到了一份工作。她……她也没给我任何地址。"他摸了摸电报。

第二天我去值班时他还在那里。他一看见我,就走了过来。

"她在哪里工作过吗?"我问。

他点了点头。"她以前是个打字员。我给她以前的老板拍了电报。他们只知道她不干了,结婚去了。"

在接下来的三四天,哈里每趟车都接了。当然,铁路方面作了例行检查,警察也介入了此事。但是实际上谁也没真正帮上忙。我看得出来,他们都觉得梅只不过是跟他开了个玩笑,但不知怎么我却从来没有这么认为过。

有一天,大约是过了两周之后,我和哈里聊天,我给他谈了我的理论。"假如你等的时间够长的话,"我说道,"总有一天,你会看见她走上楼梯的。"听罢,他转过身看着楼梯,仿佛过去从来没见过似的。

第二天我去上班时,哈里已经站在托尼杂志摊的柜台后面了。他不大好意思地看着我说,"呃,我总得在哪儿找个工作,是不是?"

于是,他开始给托尼当起了伙计。我们再也没有谈起过这事,谁也没有再提起过的我的那个理论。但是我注意到只要有人上楼,哈里总要看一眼。

到年底时,托尼由于赌博发生争执而被别人杀了。托尼的遗孀把杂志摊彻底交给了哈里打理。过了些时候,她再婚了,哈里就把杂志摊从她手里盘了过来。他借了钱,装了个冷饮柜,不久,小生意就做得红红火火。

　　这样的情况一直持续到了昨天，我听见了一声叫喊，还听见好多东西噼里啪啦掉到地上的声音。那声喊叫来自哈里，掉在地上的是一大堆玩具和其他东西，都是他跳过柜台时弄翻的。他从这些东西上面跑过去一把抓住了一个女孩，她就在离我窗户不到10英尺的地方。她个子小小的，皮肤黑黑的，眉心处有一个小点儿。

　　好一会儿的时间他们就那么待着，面对面地看着，哭着，讲些没什么意义的话。她好像说了几个词，"我指的是汽车站……"而他则把她吻得说不出话来，告诉她自己为找她所做的许多事情。显而易见，三年前梅是乘汽车而不是火车来的。她电报里指的是"汽车站"而不是"火车站"。她在汽车站等了好几天，为了找哈里，花掉了所有的钱。最后，她找了一份打字的工作。

　　"什么？"哈里说，"你在城里工作？一直都在？"

　　她点了点头。

　　"哎呀，天哪。你就从来没有来过火车站？"他把手指向杂志摊。"我一直就在那里。那个摊儿是我的。每当有人上楼，我都会仔细看。"

　　她的脸色开始变得有点儿苍白。没过多久，她向楼梯看去，声音微弱地说道："我以前从来没有上过这个楼梯。你看，我昨天出城是去办点公事，没去多长时间。噢，哈里！"然后，她伸手搂住他的脖子，真的哭了起来。

　　过了一会儿，她退后了几步，用手僵硬地指车站的最北头。"哈里，三年来，整整三年，我就在那儿，就在这个车站工作，在站长办公室里，打字。"

Detour to Romance

Located in the checkroom in Union Station as I am, I see everybody that comes up the stairs.

Harry came in a little over three years ago and waited at the head of the stairs for the passengers from the 9:05 train.

I remember seeing Harry that first evening. He wasn't much more than a thin, anxious kid then. He was all dressed up and I knew he was meeting his girl and that they would be married twenty minutes after she arrived.

Well, the passengers came up and I had to get busy. I didn't look toward the stairs again until nearly time for the 9:18 and I was very surprised to see that the young fellow was still there.

She didn't come on the 9:18 either, nor on the 9:40, and when the passengers from the 10:02 had all arrived and left, Harry was looking pretty desperate. Pretty soon he came close to my window so I called out and asked him what she looked like.

"She's small and dark," he said, "and nineteen years old and very neat in the way she walks. She has a face," he said, thinking a minute, "that has lots of spirit. I mean she can get mad but she never stays mad for long, and her eyebrows come to a little point in the middle. She's got a brown fur, but maybe she isn't wearing it."

I couldn't remember seeing anybody like that.

He showed me the telegram he'd received: Arrive thursday. Meet me station. Love love love love. May. It was from Omaha, Nebraska.

"Well," I finally said, "why don't you phone to your home? She's probably called there if she got in ahead of you."

He gave me a sick look. "I've only been in town two days. We were going to meet and then drive down South where I've got a job. She hasn't any address for me." He touched the telegram.

When I came on duty the next day he was still there and came over as soon as he saw me.

"Did she work anywhere?" I asked.

He nodded. "She was a typist. I telegraphed her former boss. All they know is that she left her job to get married."

Harry met every train for the next three or four days. Of course, the railroad lines made a routine checkup and the police looked into the case. But nobody was any real help. I could see that they all figured that May had simply played a trick on him. But I never believed that, somehow.

One day, after about two weeks, Harry and I were talking and I told him about my theory. "If you'll just wait long enough," I said, "you'll see her coming up those stairs some day." He turned and looked at the stairs as though he had never seen them before.

The next day when I came to work Harry was behind the counter of Tony's magazine stand. He looked at me rather sheepishly and said, "Well, I had to get a job somewhere, didn't I?"

So he began to work as a clerk for Tony. We never spoke of May anymore and neither of us ever mentioned my theory. But I noticed that Harry always saw every person who came up the stairs.

Toward the end of the year Tony was killed in some argument over gambling, and Tony's widow left Harry in complete charge of the magazine stand. And when she got married again some time later, Harry bought the stand from her. He borrowed money and installed a soda fountain and pretty soon he had a very nice little business.

Then came yesterday. I heard a cry and a lot of things falling. The cry was from Harry and the things falling were a lot of dolls and other things which he had upset while he was jumping over the counter. He ran across and grabbed a girl not ten feet from my window. She was small and dark and her eyebrows came to a little point in the middle.

For a while they just hung there to each other laughing and crying and saying things without meaning. She'd say a few words like, "It was the bus station I meant…" and he'd kiss her speechless and tell her the many things he had done to find her.

What apparently had happened three years before was that May had come by bus, not by train, and in her telegram she meant "bus station", not "railroad station". She had waited at the bus station for days and had spent all her money trying to find Harry. Finally she got a job typing.

"What?" said Harry. "Have you been working in town? All the time?"

She nodded.

"Well, Heavens. Didn't you ever come down here to the station?" He pointed across to his magazine stand. "I've been there all the time. I own it. I've watched everybody that came up the stairs."

She began to look a little pale. Pretty soon she looked over at the stairs and said in a weak voice, "I never came up the stairs before. You see, I went out of town yesterday on a short business trip. Oh, Harry!" Then she threw her arms around his neck and really began to cry.

After a minute she backed away and pointed very stiffly toward the north end of the station. "Harry, for three years, for three solid years, I've been right over there working right in this very station, typing, in the office of the stationmaster."

分文不取

一天晚上，我们的小男孩来到厨房，他妈妈正在那儿做晚饭。他递给妈妈一张带字的纸。妈妈在围裙上擦干手后开始读纸上的内容，只见上面写着：

割草　5美元

本周打扫自己的房间　1美元

帮你跑腿去商店买东西　50美分

当你购物时帮你照看小弟弟　25美分

倒垃圾　1美元

获得优异的成绩　5美元

清理庭院并耙草、叶　2美元

共计：14.75美元

好的，我要告诉你的是，他妈妈看到他满怀期待地站在那里，哇，好家伙，我能看到回忆一幕幕在她脑海里闪过，只见她灵机一动拿起笔来，把他写的那张纸翻过来，写下了如下文字：

我9月怀胎，让你慢慢长大，分文不取。

为你熬的那些夜,给你喂药,为你祈祷,分文不取。

多年来,为你煎熬,为你流泪,分文不取。

因可以预知的、充满恐惧和担忧的不眠之夜,分文不取。

为你买玩具、食物、衣服,还有给你擦鼻子,分文不取,孩子。

当你把所有这些全部加起时,我全部的爱,分文不取。

嗯,朋友们,当我们的孩子读完他妈妈写的这些文字以后,不禁热泪盈眶。他直视着他妈妈说道:"妈妈,我真的爱你!"然后,他拿起笔写了几个大大的字:**"一分不欠"**。

No Charge

Our little boy came up to his mother in the kitchen one evening while she was fixing supper, and handed her a piece of paper that he had been writing on. After his mom dried her hands on an apron, she read it, and this is what it said:

> For cutting the grass $5.00
> For cleaning up my room this week $1.00
> For going to the store for you $0.50
> Baby—sitting my kid brother while you went shopping $0.25
> Taking out the garbage $1.00
> For getting a good report card $5.00
> For cleaning up and raking the yard $2.00
> Total owed: $14.75

Well, I'll tell you, his mother looked at him standing there expectantly, and boy, could I see the memories flashing through her mind. So she picked up the pen, turned over the paper he'd written on, and this is what she wrote:

For the nine months I carried you while you were growing inside me, No Charge.

For all the nights that I've sat up with you, doctored and prayed for you, No Charge.

For all the trying times, and all the tears that you've caused through the years, there's No Charge.

For all the nights that were filled with dread, and for the worries I knew were ahead, No Charge.

For the toys, food, clothes, and even wiping your nose, there's No Charge, Son.

When you add it all up, the cost of my love is No Charge.

Well, friends, when our son finished reading what his mother had written, there were great big old tears in his eyes, and he looked straight up at his mother and said: "Mom, I sure do love you." And then he took the pen and in great big letters he wrote: "PAID IN FULL".

窗 外

两个身患重病的人同住一间病房。其中一个每天下午都要在病床上坐起来，把肺里的积液排出去，他的病床挨着病房里唯一的窗户。另一个人只能整天仰面朝天地平躺着。

这两个人一聊就是几个小时，他们聊自己的妻子、家人、房子、工作，在部队服役的种种，在哪里度假什么的。每天下午，靠窗的那个人需要坐起来的时候，他都会把时间花在给室友描绘他所看到的窗外的一切。另一张床上的这个人开始每天盼望着这一个小时，窗外五彩缤纷的世界、丰富多彩的活动拓宽了他的世界，让他的世界生机盎然起来。

从窗口可以俯瞰下面的一个漂亮的公园。水面上有鸭子和天鹅在嬉戏，孩子们的模型船在游弋，年轻的情人们手挽着手在彩虹般五彩斑斓的花丛中漫步，参天古树为风景增色，远处优美城市的轮廓清晰可见。每当靠窗的人详详细细地描绘着这一切的时候，房间另一头的人就会闭上眼睛，想象这如画的风景。

一个温暖的下午，靠窗的人描绘经过的一个游行队伍。虽然另一个人并没有听到乐队的声音，他却在脑海里看到了靠窗的先生绘声绘色描述的一切。

日子一天天、一星期一星期地过去了，一天早晨，值日班的护士给他们端洗澡水的时候，发现靠窗的人的身体已经没有体征了，原来他已经在睡梦之中安详地逝去了。日班护士很难过,叫来医院的护理人员把尸体抬走了。

一看时机到了,另外那个人问护士自己能否换到靠窗的床位。护士很高兴给他调换了位置,确信他很舒服了才把他一个人留在了病房。他用一个胳膊肘慢慢地痛苦地撑了起来,要向窗外看第一眼。终于可以亲眼观赏外面风景了,他心里非常高兴。他吃力地慢慢转过头来看着窗外,却发现窗外面对的是一堵墙。

这个人问护士是什么原因促使死去的室友描绘出窗外那么奇妙的种种,护士答道,那个人是个盲人,连那堵墙都看不到。她说道:"他可能只是想给你打气吧。"

A Room with a View

Two men, both seriously ill, occupied the same hospital room. One man was allowed to sit up in his bed for an hour each afternoon to help drain the fluid from his lungs. His bed was next to the room's only window. The other man had to spend all his time flat on his back.

The men talked for hours on end. They spoke of their wives and families, their homes, their jobs, their involvement in the military service, where they had been on vacation. And every afternoon when the man in the bed by the window could sit up, he would pass the time by describing to his roommate all the things he could see outside the window. The man in the other bed began to live for those one-hour periods where his world would be broadened and enlivened by all the activity and color of the world outside.

The window overlooked a park with a lovely lake. Ducks and swans played on the water while children sailed their model boats. Young lovers walked arm in arm amidst flowers of every color of the rainbow. Grand old trees graced the landscape, and a fine view of the city skyline could be seen in the distance. As the man by the window described all this in great detail, the man on the other side of the room would close his eyes and imagine the picturesque landscape.

One warm afternoon the man by the window described a parade passing by. Although the other man couldn't hear the band—he could see it in his mind's eye as the gentleman by the window describe it with descriptive words.

Days and weeks passed. One morning, the day nurse arrived to bring water for their baths only to find the lifeless body of the man by the window, who had died peacefully in his sleep. She was sad and called the hospital attendants to take the body away.

As soon as it seemed appropriate, the other man asked if he could be moved next to the window. The nurse was happy to make the switch, and after making sure he was comfortable, she left him alone. Slowly and painfully, he propped himself up on one elbow to take his first look at the world outside. Finally, he would have the joy of seeing it for himself. He strained to slowly turn to look out the window beside the bed. It faced a blank wall.

The man asked the nurse what could have compelled his deceased roommate who had described such wonderful things outside this window. The nurse responded that the man was blind and could not even see the wall. She said, "Perhaps he just wanted to encourage you."

失败意味着什么

罗伯特·哈罗德·舒勒

失败
并不意味着你就是个失败者,
它只
意味着你还不是个成功者。

失败
并不意味着你一无所获,
它只
意味着你已经有所习得。

失败
并不意味着你行事愚蠢,
它只
意味着你曾经满怀信心。

失败
并不意味着你丢人现眼,

它只
意味着曾经你敢冲敢闯。

失败
并不意味着你一事无成,
它只
意味着你需要另辟蹊径。

失败
并不意味着你比常人差,
它只
意味着你并非完美无瑕。

失败
并不意味着你虚度年华,
它只
意味着你有理由从头再来。

失败
并不意味着你应该就此放弃,
它只
意味着你将来需要加倍努力。

失败
并不意味着你此生只能是败局,

它只
意味着还需要假以时日。

失败
并不意味着你已见弃于上帝,
它只
意味着上帝有了个更好的创意。

What does Failure Mean

By Robert Harold Schuller

Failure

doesn't mean you are a failure,

It does

mean you haven't succeeded yet.

Failure

doesn't mean you have accomplished nothing,

It does mean

you have learned something.

Failure

doesn't mean you have been a fool,

It does

mean you had a lot of faith.

Failure

doesn't mean you've been disgraced,

It does

mean you were willing to try.

Failure

doesn't mean you don't have it,

It does

mean you have to do something in a different way.

Failure

doesn't mean you are inferior,

It does

mean you are not perfect.

Failure

doesn't mean you've wasted your life,

It does

mean you have a reason to start afresh.

Failure

doesn't mean you should give up,

It does

mean you must try harder.

Failure

doesn't mean you'll never make it,

It does

mean it will take a little longer.

Failure

doesn't mean God has abandoned you,

It does

mean God has a better idea.

加利福尼亚的传说

我年轻的时候,曾经去加利福尼亚淘过金,尽管我没有淘到足够的金子让自己一夜暴富,却发现了一处世外桃源。那个地方叫作"斯坦尼斯洛",它宛如人间天堂,重峦叠嶂,青山密林,林中有风轻轻拂过树枝。

多年以前,在我还没到这里的时候,就已经有人来加利福尼亚斯坦尼斯洛的青山密林里淘金了。他们在山谷里建造了一座小镇,盖起了漂亮的家庭小房子,镇里还有人行道、商店、银行、学校,设施齐全。

起初,他们在斯坦尼斯洛山上淘到了许多金子,可惜好景不长,几年后,金子却再也淘不到了。等我到了斯坦尼斯洛的时候,大家已经走得差不多了。

如今,小镇的街道上荒草丛生,小房子都被野玫瑰丛所掩。多年前的那个夏天,当我走在空无一人的小镇上时,只能听到遍地的虫鸣声,就在那时,我突然发觉,除了我之外,还有人。

一个男人站在一栋小房子前向我微笑,这间房子没有被野玫瑰丛所掩,房子前面有片漂亮的小花园,里面种满了花,有蓝色的,还有黄色的。房子的窗户上挂着白色窗帘,在夏日和煦的微风中,窗帘随风飘动。

他的脸上还挂着笑,打开门示意我进去。我进了屋,眼前的景象令人难以置信。之前几周,我和其他采矿工人住在简陋的矿营里。我们睡在坚硬的地上,吃着冰冷的金属碟子里的罐头豆子,整日艰难地寻找着金子。

此刻,在这间小小的房子里,我再一次元气满满了。

我看到:擦得锃亮的木地板上铺了一块艳丽的地毯,房间四壁挂满了画,小台桌上摆放着一些海贝壳、书籍和插满了鲜花的瓷花瓶。我想,是他太太把这幢房子装扮得温馨如家吧。

一定是因为我喜形于色,他看出了我的心思,"是的,"他微笑着对我说,"一切都是她的杰作,家里每一处都是她亲手布置的。"

墙上有幅画挂歪了,他发现了,走过去正过来,他后退了几次,确保画真的挂正了,然后他用手轻轻碰了碰画。

"她总是这样,"他向我解释道,"就像母亲给她的孩子梳完头最后总要拍一下,我常常看到她整理这些东西,现在我已经模仿得惟妙惟肖了,我不知道自己为什么会这样,我只是下意识地这样。"

他说这些话的时候,我突然意识到,他是想要让我留意到这间房子里的某些东西。于是,我环顾四周,当我目光落到屋里壁炉旁的一个角落的时候,他突然开心地大笑起来,激动地搓着双手。

"就是它!"他喊道,"你终于发现了!我就知道你会发现的!那是她的照片。"我走过去,看到一个黑色小架子上,摆放着一张小照片,照片里的女人是我见过的最美的女人,表情里有着我从未见过的甜美温柔。

他从我手中拿过照片,目不转睛地看着,嘴里说道,"这是在她上次过十九岁生日的时候照的,那天我们喜结良缘,等你看到她……哦,等等,只要你见到她就什么都知道了!"

"她现在在哪里?"我问道。

"哦,她出门了,"他叹了口气,把照片放回到黑色小架子上,"她回娘家看望父母去了,他们住的地方离这里有四五十英里,到今天她已经走了两个星期了。"

"她什么时候回来呀?"我问道。"嗯,今天是周三,"他不紧不慢地说道,"她周六晚上回来。"

我感到非常失望,我说道,"很遗憾,那时我也已经走了。"

"走了?不!为什么你要走?不要走!她会感到十分遗憾的。你看,她喜欢有客人来和我们住在一起。"

"不了,我真的必须要离开了。"我坚定地说道。

他把那张照片拿起来,放在我面前,"看这里,"他说道,"现在,你当着她的面告诉她,你本来可以留下来和她见面,可是你不愿意。"

我再一次看了看这张照片,随即改变了主意,我决定留下来。

他告诉我,他叫亨利。

当晚,亨利和我谈到了许多事情,不过大部分都与她相关。次日,时间悄然流逝。

周四晚上,来了一位访客。他名叫汤姆,是一名身材高大、白发苍苍的矿工,"打扰您几分钟,我只是来问问,她什么时候会回家。"他进一步解释道。"有新的消息吗?"

"嗯,有消息,"亨利回答道。"我收到一封信,你们想听听吗?"亨利从衬衫口袋里掏出一个泛黄的信封,给我们读起来。这封信里写满了对他,还有对他们的好朋友和邻居的深情厚谊。亨利读完了信,望向汤姆,"噢,不要这样!你又来了,汤姆!每次我读她的信你都会哭,这次我要把这件事告诉她!"

"不要,你千万不要这样,亨利!"白发苍苍的矿工说道,"我老了,多愁善感,我多么希望她今晚就在这里。"

第二天，周五，又有一名老矿工登门拜访。他请求亨利读一下她的来信，深情的信也让他泪流满面。"我们也都非常想念她。"他说道。周六终于来临了。我不停地看表。亨利注意到了，他问我，"你不会以为她出事了吧，是吗？"

我笑了笑说我肯定她一切安好，但是亨利似乎并不满足。

夕阳西下的时候，亨利的朋友汤姆和乔沿着小路走来，看到他们我非常高兴。老矿工们带着吉他、鲜花和一瓶威士忌。他们把花插进花瓶里，然后开始用吉他弹奏欢快活泼的乐曲。

亨利的朋友们不停地递给他一杯又一杯威士忌让他喝，我看到桌子上还剩下两杯酒，于是伸手去拿其中一杯，汤姆抓住我的胳膊，低声说道："放下那杯，拿另外一杯。"午夜的钟声敲响了，他把剩下的那杯威士忌酒递给亨利。

亨利一饮而尽。他的脸变得越来越苍白，"老兄们，"他说道，"我感觉不太舒服，我要躺一下。"

话刚出口，他就沉沉地睡着了。

两个朋友立刻抬起他，把他抬进卧室里，他们关上门，然后退了出来。看起来他们似乎要离开了，于是我急忙说道："请别离开，先生们，她不认识我，我对她来说只是陌生人。"

他们面面相觑，汤姆说道："他太太十九年前就去世了。"

"去世了？"目瞪口呆的我屏息问道。

"也许去世了，也许情况更糟。"他答道。

"那是六月的一个周六晚上，他们婚后六个月左右，她回娘家探望父母，她快到家时，在路上被印第安人绑架了，从那以后就再也没人见过她。亨利疯了，他觉得她还活着。每到六月，他就会发作，以为妻子回家看望父母了，他会一直等她回来，时不时拿出那封发黄的信，我们去看望他，让他读给我们听。"

"此后，每年六月那个周六晚上，也就是她本该回来的那个晚上，我们都会过来陪他，在他酒里面加安眠药，让他能睡过这一晚，然后他就会平安度过新的一年。"

乔拿起帽子和吉他说道："十九年间，每到六月，我们都会这么做。第一年的时候，我们一共有二十七个人，现在只剩我们两个了。"说完，他打开门，两位老人渐渐消失在斯坦尼斯洛茫茫的黑夜里。

The Californian's Tale

When I was young, I went looking for gold in California. I never found enough to make me rich. But I did discover a beautiful part of the country. It was called "the Stanislau". The Stanislau was like Heaven on Earth. It had bright green hills and deep forests where soft winds touched the trees.

Other men, also looking for gold, had reached the Stanislau hills of California many years before I did. They had built a town in the valley with sidewalks and stores, banks and schools. They had also built pretty little houses for their families.

At first, they found a lot of gold in the Stanislau hills. But their good luck did not last. After a few years, the gold disappeared. By the time I reached the Stanislau, all the people were gone, too.

Grass now grew in the streets. And the little houses were covered by wild rose bushes. Only the sound of insects filled the air as I walked through the empty town that summer day so long ago. Then, I realized I was not alone after all.

A man was smiling at me as he stood in front of one of the little houses. This house was not covered by wild rose bushes. A nice little garden in front of the house was full of blue and yellow flowers. White curtains hung from the windows and floated in the soft summer wind.

Still smiling, the man opened the door of his house and motioned to me. I went inside and could not believe my eyes. I had been living for weeks in rough mining camps with other gold miners. We slept on the hard ground, ate canned beans from cold metal plates and spent our days in the difficult search for gold.

Here in this little house, my spirit seemed to come to life again.

I saw a bright rug on the shining wooden floor. Pictures hung all around the room. And on little tables there were seashells, books and china vases full of flowers. A woman had made this house into a home.

The pleasure I felt in my heart must have shown on my face. The man read my thoughts. "Yes," he smiled, "it is all her work. Everything in this room has felt the touch of her hand."

One of the pictures on the wall was not hanging straight. He noticed it and went to fix it. He stepped back several times to make sure the picture was really straight. Then he gave it a gentle touch with his hand.

"She always does that," he explained to me. "It is like the finishing pat a mother gives her child's hair after she has brushed it. I have seen her fix all these things so often that I can do it just the way she does. I don't know why I do it. I just do it."

As he talked, I realized there was something in this room that he wanted me to discover. I looked around. When my eyes reached a corner of the room near the fireplace, he broke into a happy laugh and rubbed his hands together.

"That's it!" he cried out. "You have found it! I knew you would. It is her picture." I went to a little black shelf that held a small picture of the most beautiful woman I had ever seen. There was a sweetness and softness in the woman's expression that I had never seen before.

The man took the picture from my hands and stared at it. "She was nineteen on her last birthday. That was the day we were married. When you see her…oh, just wait until you meet her!"

"Where is she now?" I asked.

"Oh, she is away," the man sighed, putting the picture back on the little black shelf. "She went to visit her parents. They live forty or fifty miles from here. She has been gone two weeks today."

"When will she be back?" I asked. "Well, this is Wednesday," he said slowly. "She will be back on Saturday, in the evening."

I felt a sharp sense of regret. "I am sorry, because I will be gone by then." I said.

"Gone? No! Why should you go? Don't go. She will be

so sorry. You see, she likes to have people come and stay with us."

"No, I really must leave." I said firmly.

He picked up her picture and held it before my eyes. "Here," he said. "Now you tell her to her face that you could have stayed to meet her and you would not."

Something made me change my mind as I looked at the picture for a second time. I decided to stay.

The man told me his name was Henry.

That night, Henry and I talked about many different things, but mainly about her. The next day passed quietly.

Thursday evening we had a visitor. He was a big, grey-haired miner named Tom. "I just came for a few minutes to ask when she is coming home," he explained. "Is there any news?"

"Oh yes," the man replied. "I got a letter. Would you like to hear it?" He took a yellowed letter out of his shirt pocket and read it to us. It was full of loving messages to him and to other people—their close friends and neighbors. When the man finished reading it, he looked at his friend. "Oh no, you are doing it again, Tom! You always cry when I read a letter from her. I'm going to tell her this time!"

"No, you must not do that, Henry," the grey-haired miner said. "I am getting old. And any little sorrow makes me cry. I really was hoping she would be here tonight."

The next day, Friday, another old miner came to visit. He asked to hear the letter. The message in it made him cry, too. "We all miss her so much, " he said. Saturday finally came. I found I was looking at my watch very often. Henry noticed this. "You don't think something has happened to her, do you? " he asked me.

I smiled and said that I was sure she was just fine. But he did not seem satisfied.

I was glad to see his two friends, Tom and Joe, coming down the road as the sun began to set. The old miners were carrying guitars. They also brought flowers and a bottle of whiskey. They put the flowers in vases and began to play some fast and lively songs on their guitars.

Henry's friends kept giving him glasses of whiskey, which they made him drink. When I reached for one of the two glasses left on the table, Tom stopped my arm. "Drop that glass and take the other one!" he whispered. He gave the remaining glass of whiskey to Henry just as the clock began to strike midnight.

Henry emptied the glass. His face grew whiter and whiter. "Boys, " he said, "I am feeling sick. I want to lie down."

Henry was asleep almost before the words were out of his mouth.

In a moment, his two friends had picked him up and carried him into the bedroom. They closed the door and came back. They seemed to be getting ready to leave. So I said, "Please don't go gentlemen. She will not know me. I am a stranger to her."

They looked at each other. "His wife has been dead for nineteen years," Tom said.

"Dead?" I whispered.

"Dead or worse," he said.

"She went to see her parents about six months after she got married. On her way back, on a Saturday evening in June, when she was almost here, the Indians captured her. No one ever saw her again. Henry lost his mind. He thinks she is still alive. When June comes, he thinks she has gone on her trip to see her parents. Then he begins to wait for her to come back. He gets out that old letter. And we come around to visit so he can read it to us."

"On the Saturday night she is supposed to come home, we come here to be with him. We put a sleeping drug in his drink so he will sleep through the night. Then he is all right for another year."

Joe picked up his hat and his guitar. "We have done this every June for nineteen years," he said. "The first year there were twenty-seven of us. Now just the two of us are left." He opened the door of the pretty little house. And the two old men disappeared into the darkness of the Stanislau.

浮生半日

我走到爸爸身旁,紧紧地抓住了他的右手。我浑身上下都换上了新装:黑色的鞋、绿色的校服、红色的帽子,可我却高兴不起来,因为这是我被扔进学校的第一天。

我妈妈站在窗前看着我们的进展,我三步一回头地看着她,巴望着她能来帮帮我。我们沿着一条街道往前走,街道两边都是果园和田地,地里种着庄稼:梨树和枣树。

"为什么叫我去上学?"我问爸爸。"我犯了什么错?"

"我这不是在罚你,"他哈哈大笑,解释道,"上学不是一种惩罚,学校是把小男孩培养成有用的大人的地方。你难道不想像你的几个哥哥那样成为有用的人吗?"

听了这些话,我却没有被说服,我不相信把我从家里拽出来扔进那个四周都是高墙的大房子里有什么用。

我们来到学校的大门口,能看到里面那个宽敞的大院里都是男孩和女孩。"你自己进去吧,"我爸爸说道,"去跟他们在一起。乐呵呵地,给他们树立一个好榜样。"

我犹豫起来,紧紧地抓着爸爸的手,可是他却轻轻地把我推开。"像个堂堂的男子汉,"他说道,"你的人生从今天才真正开始。放学时,我会来这儿接你的。"

我往前走了几步,男孩和女孩的脸进入了我的视线,我却一个也不认识,他们中间也没有一个人认识我,我感觉自己是一个迷路的陌生人。不过,有几个男孩开始好奇地打量我,而其中有一个还走到我跟前问我,"谁带你来的呀?"

"我爸。"我低声答道。

"我爸死了。"他轻描淡写地说。

我不知道如何应答。这时,学校的大门关上了,一些孩子哇的一声哭了起来。铃声大作,一位女士走了过来,后面跟着一些男士。那些男士开始把我们分成一排一排的,我们在高楼环伺的大院里被分成了复杂的队列。那些高楼的每一层都有长长的木顶阳台,在那里,可以俯瞰我们。

"这里是你们的新家,"那位女士说道。"这里也有爸爸和妈妈。这里的一切都有趣又有益,所以,擦干眼泪,快乐地面对生活吧。"

好啦,原来我的疑虑都是胡思乱想。我一开始就交了许多朋友,还爱上了许多女孩,我以前根本没料到学校生活会这么多姿多彩。

我们做各种各样的游戏。我们在音乐课教室第一次唱了歌。我们还上了第一堂语文课。我们看到了地球仪,地球仪会转动,会显示各大洲和各个国家。我们开始学算术,还听了造物主的故事。我们中午吃美味可口的食物,然后是短暂的午休,醒来后继续结交朋友、谈情说爱、嬉戏玩耍、学习功课。

可是,我们的路并不全是甜蜜,没有阴霾的。我们需要会观察,有耐性,上学绝对不是嬉戏玩耍和到处闲逛,同学之间的竞争会带来痛苦、仇恨,甚至拳脚相向。虽然那位女士有时面带微笑,她也时常高声喊叫、厉声斥责,更多的时候还会对我们进行体罚。

再说,现在改变主意为时已晚,没有机会了,不可能回到天堂的家里去了。摆在我们面前的只有努力、奋斗和坚持。能抓住机遇、能力超群的同学才能获得随之而来的成功和幸福。

铃声响了,宣告一天的时间和一天的学习结束了。学校的再次大门打开,孩子们冲了过去。我对朋友们和爱人们说再见,走出了学校的大门。我环顾四周,却没有爸爸的身影,可是他答应我会在这里接我的。我站在一旁等。我等了好长时间,可他还是没有来,于是我决定自己回家。我刚走几步,就大吃一惊停了下来,我的天哪!两边都是果园的那条街怎么不见了?跑哪儿去了?满大街的小汽车是哪儿来的?这些人又都是什么时候跑到街上休息的?这些堆积如山的垃圾是怎么占据街道两旁的?街道两旁的田地到哪里去了?取而代之的是高楼大厦,满大街的孩子和空中震耳欲聋的噪音。杂耍艺人四处可见,他们在变魔术、从筐里变出蛇来。接下来,那里有个乐队奏响了马戏的开场曲,那些小丑和大力士登台亮相。

天哪!我感到头晕目眩,天旋地转,我快要疯了。浮生半日,晨昏之间,何以至此?我要回家问爸爸这是怎么了。可是我的家在哪里?我急急忙忙地向十字路口走去,因为我还记得要穿过这条街才能回家。可是车水马龙,川流不息。我怒火中烧,不知道什么时候才能过去。

我站了很长时间,最后街角熨衣店的小伙计向我走了过来。

他伸出了胳膊,说道,"老大爷,我扶你过去吧。"

Half a Day

I walked alongside my father, clutching his right hand. All my clothes were new: the black shoes, the green school uniform, and the red cap. They did not make me happy, however, as this was the day I was to be thrown into school for the first time.

My mother stood at the window watching our progress, and I turned towards her from time to time, hoping she would help. We walked along a street lined with gardens, and fields planted with crops: pears and date palms.

"Why school?" I asked my father. "What have I done?"

"I'm not punishing you," he said, laughing. "School's not a punishment. It's a place that makes useful men out of boys. Don't you want to be useful like your brothers?"

I was not convinced. I did not believe there was really any good to be had in tearing me away from my home and throwing me into the huge, high-walled building.

When we arrived at the gate we could see the courtyard, vast and full of boys and girls. "Go in by yourself," said my father, "and join them. Put a smile on your face and be a good example to others."

I hesitated and clung to his hand, but he gently pushed me from him. "Be a man," he said. "Today you truly begin life. You will find me waiting for you when it's time to leave."

I took a few steps. Then the faces of the boys and girls came into view. I did not know a single one of them, and none of them knew me. I felt I was a stranger who had lost his way. But then some boys began to glance at me in curiosity, and one of them came over and asked, "Who brought you?"

"My father," I whispered.

"My father's dead," he said simply.

I did not know what to say. The gate was now closed. Some of the children burst into tears. The bell rang. A lady came along, followed by a group of men. The men began sorting us into ranks. We were formed into an intricate pattern in the great courtyard surrounded by high buildings; from each floor we were overlooked by a long balcony roofed in wood.

"This is your new home," said the woman. "There are mothers and fathers here, too. Everything that is enjoyable and beneficial is here. So dry your tears and face life joyfully."

Well, it seemed that my misgivings had had no basis. From the first moments I made many friends and fell in love with many girls. I had never imagined school would have this rich variety of experiences.

We played all sorts of games. In the music room we sang our first songs. We also had our first introduction to language. We saw a globe of the Earth, which revolved and showed the various continents and countries. We started learning numbers, and we were told the story of the Creator of the universe. We ate delicious food, took a little nap, and woke up to go on with friendship and love, playing and learning.

Our path, however, was not totally sweet and unclouded. We had to be observant and patient. It was not all a matter of playing and fooling around. Rivalries could bring about pain and hatred or give rise to fighting. And while the lady would sometimes smile, she would often yell and scold. Even more frequently she would resort to physical punishment.

In addition, the time for changing one's mind was over and gone and there was no question of ever returning to the paradise of home. Nothing lay ahead of us but exertion, struggle, and perseverance. Those who were able took advantage of the opportunities for success and happiness that presented themselves.

The bell rang, announcing the passing of the day and the end of work. The children rushed toward the gate, which was opened again. I said goodbye to friends and sweethearts and passed through the gate. I looked around but found no trace of my father, who had promised to be there. I stepped aside to wait. When I had waited for a long time in vain, I decided to return home on my own. I walked a few steps, then came to a startled halt. Good Lord! Where was the street lined with gardens? Where had it disappeared to? When did all these cars invade it? And when did all these people come to rest on its surface? How did these hills of rubbish find their way to cover its sides? And where were the fields that bordered it? High buildings had taken over, the street was full of children, and disturbing noises shook the air. Here and there stood conjurers showing off their tricks or making snakes appear from baskets. Then there was a band announcing the opening of a circus, with clowns and weight lifters walking in front.

Good God! I was in a daze. My head spun. I almost went crazy. How could all this have happened in half a day, between early morning and sunset? I would find the answer at home with my father. But where was my home? I hurried towards the crossroads, because I remembered that I had to cross the street to reach our house, but the stream of cars would not let up. Extremely irritated, I wondered when I would be able to cross.

I stood there a long time, until the young boy employed at the ironing shop on the corner came up to me.

He stretched out his arm and said, "Grandpa, let me take you across."

写给在天堂的妻子的信

克里斯蒂安·斯普拉格的妻子乔安妮生产的时候,他们一直都处在兴奋之中……这种状态一直持续到她几小时后去世为止。克里斯蒂安在这封令人潸然泪下的信中讲述了为什么他要女儿伊尔伦了解妈妈的一切。

我亲爱的乔安妮,

我至今还记得我们的女儿出生的一个月前我们俩的对话。

你突然问我,万一你有什么不测的话,我会怎么照顾她。我记得当时对你说别犯傻了,可你却一脸认真地说道:"我只是想要你经常提醒她妈妈爱她有多深。"

"还要告诉她我是一个什么样的人。一定要让她干净整洁,多吃菜!"我现在很庆幸曾经跟你有过这场对话,我也希望自己所做的一切如你所愿。

我是多么希望你能在这里与我们共享你被带走以后的所有特殊时刻啊。

现在,对于我来说,我们共处的时光弥足珍贵。

以前,每当我说起我对你一见钟情的时候,你就会笑盈盈的,而我说的却是实话。那天我在夜店遇见你,最后终于鼓足勇气问能否请你喝一杯。当你说可以的时候,我都不敢相信我的运气会这么好。

我在威尼斯向你求婚。

我们坐威尼斯小划船贡多拉,一路上笑语盈盈。我还记得,你仰起头看着太阳,说这是你一生中最幸福的时光。而当你步入教堂向圣坛走去的时候,我意识到我迎娶的是我的灵魂伴侣,我的"唯一"。

发现你怀孕的时候,我们欣喜若狂,不久还得知是个女孩。我们进行了长达几个月的产前准备。

每次我们的小宝宝踢你的时候,你就会抓住我的手放到你的肚子上,说,"你能感觉到她吗,克里斯蒂安?她可真是活泼好动啊!"

你想给我们的女儿取名伊尔伦,跟我们在威尼斯认识的一位亲戚同名。你发现这个名字在拉丁语里的意思是"永远快乐"。

我们在伊尔伦出生前就看见她了,我们做过一个彩超,可以看到宝宝的脸,她很美。

现在,我很庆幸我们有过这一举措。当你超过了预产期两个星期还没出生的时候,我们家附近的医院向要给你引产,对于接下来将会发生的事情想都不敢想。

在伊尔伦快要出生的时候,助产士让你用力,可是伊尔伦的心律骤降——她有生命危险。

你看着我,目光里全是恐惧,我们被医生们围得里三层外三层的,他们都在想方设法地给伊尔伦接生。她生下来的时候浑身青紫,护士们飞快地把她抱进了婴儿特护恒温箱。你大声尖叫道,"她没事吧?"而我能说的只有:"没事,她很美,跟你一模一样。"

想到你都没见你的女儿一面,更不用说抱她一下,我不由得肝肠寸断。接下来,你的心律开始加快,血压开始下降,医生们说必须马上把你转移到手术室。

他们把你往外推的时候,我抓住你的脚,说"我爱你",这一别竟是永诀。

几分钟以后,一个医生把我拉到一旁,告诉我伊尔伦有重型颅脑损伤的迹象,他们觉得她生命垂危。你们俩,我都不知道要顾谁好了。

我去看恒温箱里的她。半小时以后,医生们告诉我一个消息,这个消息永远地改变了我的生活:你心脏停搏,医生要给你手术,却出现了大出血。

我的世界瞬间崩塌了,我记得我当时大声喊道:"为什么?"

你才27岁,身体再健康不过了,可你现在却去了,动脉瘤引起大出血。

谁都无法预料。医生们都尽力了。你在太平间里宛若安静地熟睡一般,我吻着你的脸颊,抚摸着你的秀发,泪如雨下。

我感觉彻底迷失了。接着,一个护士过来找我,说发生了奇迹一类的话,把我带到了伊尔伦身旁。她胸上、鼻子里、嘴里的管子都已经拔掉了,她在自己呼吸,护士说这是个奇迹。

看起来我们的伊尔伦是下定决心要活下来。一个护士把她放进我怀里,伊尔伦哭了起来。"不怕,爸爸在这儿。"我安慰她,她立刻止住了哭声。

我们的女儿要活下来了。

就好像你对上帝这样说了一样,"你可以把我带走,可是你不能把我的女儿带走。"

突然之间，我从生无可恋变成了拥有伊尔伦，我给她换第一块尿片，冲第一瓶奶——我做这些的时候心里想着你会怎么做，尽量做得跟你一样好。

可是，接下来，我回到了严酷的现实面前——你的葬礼。

有四百人参加了你的葬礼，三年前给我们证婚的牧师主持了你的葬礼。

两天后我把伊尔伦从医院接回家中。

那天夜里，我躺在我们的床上，伊尔伦躺在我们身边的小床上。我对你说，"乔，你应该在这里，我需要你。"我万念俱灰，多希望你躺在我身旁啊！

我白天以泪洗面，晚上就一定会把伊尔伦放在我身旁，给她讲述你的种种：你是多么美丽、优秀和善良。

家里到处都摆放着你的照片，我会抱着伊尔伦贴近这些照片，这样她就能看见你了。

等她一点点长大了，我会做其他事情，目的就是把你带进她的生活。我努力去烹调我知道的你会烹调的食物，好让我们美丽的伊尔伦了解她的妈妈，尽管她并不记得你的模样。

我希望你能听到我说的话，"我思念你乔安妮，不过谢谢你给予我的——我们美丽的女儿。"我只希望你在这里，享受有女儿的感觉。

伊尔伦一岁的时候，诊断出患有脑瘫，这意味着她不大可能会走路，永远也不会说话利索，需要定期护理治疗。我就是从那时候振作起来的，因为我需要竭尽全力给伊尔伦最好的生活。

尽管困难重重，却也还是奇妙无比，我们是两个小伙伴。现在，她已经快四岁了，看起来跟你一模一样。

而且她非常美丽！虽然她只会说几个词——"你好"是她的最爱——而她给了我那么多的挚爱亲情。她真是个为所欲为的小家伙，把我搞得百依百顺。

我放弃了区域销售经理的工作，这样就可以把所有的时间都给伊尔伦了。她每天上午都要参加彩虹屋的活动，那是为她这样的孩子专门设立的机构。

我每次看到她，都会得到安慰，因为她是你——乔安妮活生生的一部分，是你的传奇。

我只想要你知道，不论遭遇什么，我都会把以让你自豪的方式，把伊尔伦抚养成人，那就是——她永远都会牢记她的妈妈有多特别。

我爱你，我亲爱的，
克里斯蒂安

A Letter to His Wife in Paradise

When Christian Spragg's wife Joanne gave birth they were full of excitement…until she died just hours later. In a moving letter, Christian tells why he'll make sure their daughter Ilaria knows all about her mum.

My darling Joanne,

I still remember the conversation we had just a month before our baby daughter Ilaria was born.

Out of the blue you asked me how I'd look after her if anything happened to you. I remember telling you not to be silly but you were serious. "I'd just want you to tell her often how much her mummy loved her," you said.

"And to tell her what sort of person I was. And make sure she's clean and tidy and eats her vegetables!" Now I'm so glad we had that conversation. And I hope I've done things as you wanted.

I just wish with all my heart that you were here to enjoy all the special moments we've shared since you were taken from us.

The memories of our time together are so treasured for me now.

You used to laugh when I said I fell in love with you the moment we met but I did. I saw you in a nightclub and finally gathered the courage to ask if you'd like a drink. I couldn't believe my luck when you said yes.

I asked you to be my wife in Venice.

We splashed out on a gondola ride, giggling to ourselves. I remember you tilted your head up to the sun and told me that this was one of the best days of your life. And when you walked down the aisle I knew I'd married my soulmate, "the one".

When we found out you were pregnant we were ecstatic and soon we discovered it was a girl and spent the months running up to the birth getting the nursery ready.

Every time our baby kicked you'd grab my hand, put it on your tummy and say, "Can you feel her Christian? She's so lively!"

You wanted to call our daughter Ilaria after a family friend you'd met in Venice. You found out that in Latin it meant "always happy".

We saw Ilaria before she was born. We had a 3D scan where you can see your baby's face—she was beautiful.

I am so thankful we did that now. When you went two weeks past your due date the hospital near our home in Bolton wanted to induce you. It's hard for me to think straight about what happened next.

When Ilaria was ready to come the midwife told you to push but Ilaria's heartbeat dropped—she was in distress.

You looked at me in terror as we were surrounded by doctors trying to get Ilaria out. When she was born she was blue and nurses rushed her to the special care baby unit. You screamed, "Is she OK?" and all I could say was, "Yes, she's beautiful, just like you."

It breaks my heart you never even saw your daughter, let alone held her. Then your heart rate started going up and your blood pressure started going down. Doctors said they had to get you into theatre straight away.

As they wheeled you out I grabbed your foot and said "I love you". It was the last time I saw you alive.

Minutes later a doctor took me aside and told me Ilaria was showing signs of major brain damage and they didn't expect her to live. I didn't know which of you to turn to first.

I went to see Ilaria in her incubator. Half an hour later doctors told me the news that would change my life forever. There had been massive bleeding and as they tried to operate you'd had a cardiac arrest.

My world fell apart. I remember shouting, "Why?"

You were just 27, healthy as can be, and now you were gone. An aneurysm had caused the bleeding.

No-one could have foreseen it, the doctors did all they could. In the chapel of rest you looked like you were sleeping peacefully. I kissed your face and stroked your hair as I sobbed.

I felt totally lost. Then a nurse came to find me and said something amazing had happened and led me to Ilaria. She'd pulled all the tubes out of her chest and nose and was breathing on her own. The nurses said it was a miracle.

It seemed our Ilaria was determined to stay alive. A nurse laid her in my arms and she began to cry. "Don't worry, Daddy's here." I told her, and she immediately stopped crying.

Our daughter was going to live.

It was as if you'd said, "God, you can have me, but you're not having my daughter."

Suddenly, from feeling I had nothing left to live for, I had Ilaria. I changed her first nappy, gave her her first bottle—I thought about how you'd have done it and tried to do it the same way.

But then it was back to the terrible reality—your funeral.

Four hundred people attended as the vicar who'd married us buried you just three years later.

And then, two days later I brought Ilaria home from the hospital.

That first night I lay in our bed, Ilaria beside me in her cot and I talked to you. "Jo, you should be here, I need you," I said. I so desperately wished you were lying beside me.

I spent my days in tears. At night I'd lay Ilaria next to me and tell her about you—how, beautiful, good and kind you were.

Photos of you were all over the house and I'd hold Ilaria close to them so she could see you.

And as she gets older, I do other things to bring you into her life. I try to cook things I know you'd have made to make our beautiful Ilaria know her mum, even if she doesn't remember you.

I hope you can hear me when I say: "I miss you Joanne but thank you for our wonderful daughter." I just wish you were here to enjoy her.

When Ilaria was a year old she was diagnosed with cerebral palsy which means she is unlikely to walk. She'll never speak properly and will require constant care. That's when I pulled myself together. I needed to, to give Ilaria the best life I can.

Although it's hard it's wonderful too, we're like two little mates. She's nearly four now and looks just like you.

And what a personality. Although she can only say a few words—"Hiya!" is her favourite—she gives me so much love and affection. She's a real cheeky little thing, and can wrap me right round her little finger.

I gave up my job as an area sales manager so that I could devote my time to Ilaria. Every morning she attends Rainbow House, where they specialise in helping children like her.

Every time I look at her I get comfort because she's a living part of you Joanne, your legacy.

I just want you to know that whatever happens I will bring up Ilaria in a way you would have been proud of—and she will always know how special her mummy was.

         I love you my darling,
             Christian

图书在版编目（CIP）数据

生命中一直在等待的那一天：英汉对照 /（美）弗罗伊德·戴尔等著；张白桦译. —北京：中国国际广播出版社，2018.4（2019.1重印）
（译趣坊. 世界微型小说精选）
ISBN 978-7-5078-4276-0

Ⅰ. ①生… Ⅱ. ①弗… ②张… Ⅲ. ①小小说－小说集－美国－现代－英、汉 Ⅳ. ①I712.45

中国版本图书馆CIP数据核字（2018）第065152号

生命中一直在等待的那一天（中英双语）

著　　者	[美] 弗罗伊德·戴尔 等
译　　者	张白桦
策　　划	张娟平
责任编辑	笑学婧
版式设计	国广设计室
责任校对	徐秀英

出版发行	中国国际广播出版社 [010-83139469　010-83139489(传真)]
社　　址	北京市西城区天宁寺前街2号北院A座一层
	邮编：100055
网　　址	www.chirp.com.cn
经　　销	新华书店
印　　刷	环球东方（北京）印务有限公司

开　本	880×1230　1/32
字　数	200千字
印　张	6.5
版　次	2018年5月　北京第一版
印　次	2019年1月　第二次印刷
定　价	26.00元

欢迎关注本社新浪官方微博
官方网站 www.chirp.cn

版权所有
盗版必究